3 1111 01232 0493

D0464968

Collecting
and
Identifying
Old
Clocks

Books by H.G. Harris

Handbook of Watch and Clock Repairs
Advanced Watch and Clock Repair

COLLECTING
and
IDENTIFYING
OLD
CLOCKS

H.G. HARRIS

1977

EMERSON BOOKS, INC.
BUCHANAN, NEW YORK 10511

CONTENTS

Preface

Chapter

Appendix

Index

PREFACE

COLLECTING old clocks is a very interesting and instructive hobby and at the same time can be financially rewarding, but some basic knowledge is needed with which to start. It is for that purpose that this book has been written.

As with period furniture, old clocks have come to be regarded as collector's pieces and, like any other antique, they have a commercial value. In the establishments of qualified dealers and in the salesroom of prominent auctioneers, antique clocks are frequently sold for between $1,000 and $16,000. Recently, at a leading London auction a French carriage clock brought $35,000.

Dealing in clocks of such high value is an occupation only for dealers and wealthy collectors, but there must be a vast number of clocks in the world today just waiting to be 'discovered'. Clocks that for years have remained hidden in old buildings, cupboards, chests, attics, cabins, barns and sheds that, for one reason or another, were discarded by their owners. Perhaps the clock was considered noisy, or it just stopped, or the owner tired of it; but no matter what the reason these clocks are sure to have a value of some kind.

There is of course always the possibility of finding old clocks in secondhand shops and junk shops, particularly in out-of-the-way towns. However, one needs to know whether the price is reasonable or ridiculous.

The value of a clock is dependent on a number of factors such as type, age, maker, complicated work and condition. These points are dealt with in the appropriate chapters, sufficiently to enable a beginner to decide whether or not a clock is likely to have value as an antique. In this respect the notes in Chapter 10, while being written with grandfather clocks in mind, will nevertheless be helpful when assessing most old domestic clocks. Dates can only be approximate unless reference is to a specific event, and they are, therefore, preceded by circa or c meaning 'about'.

There are two very excellent associations that provide helpful services to collectors of clocks and watches. Details of membership and activities may be obtained by writing to the following addresses:

National Association of Watch and Clock Collectors, Inc.
P.O. Box 33
Columbia, Pa. 17512

The Antiquarian Horological Society
New House
High Street
Ticehurst
Wadhurst
Sussex, TN5 7AL, England

It is sincerely hoped that this book will help you to recognize a collector's piece and possibly enable you to start a collection of your own.

H.G. Harris

CHAPTER I

Primitive Time Indicators

IF a short stick is placed vertically in the ground in a sunny position the longest shadows will be at sunrise and sunset, and the shortest shadow will be observed at midday when the sun is at its meridian, i.e. at its maximum height.

If these three positions are marked, and the two distances so formed are further divided, the device will provide a visual indication of how much daylight time has passed since sunrise and how much is left before sunset. The positions of these marks will vary according to the distance that separates the locality from the equator. The distance is expressed geographically as latitude, and is measured in degrees north or south of the equator. The imaginary lines of latitude are those which circumvent the earth parallel to the equator.

Such devices were known as shadow-clocks and were used by Babylonians and Egyptians as far back as 1000 B.C., possibly even earlier.

This primitive but effective method of tracking the progress of the sun across the sky was the forerunner of the sundial, but without the sun there were no shadow readings and therein lay their disadvantage.

The clepsydra, or water-clock, was also being used in Egypt at this time and there is evidence to suggest they were in existence about 1400 B.C. In principle they were conical containers filled with water that was allowed to leak away at

9

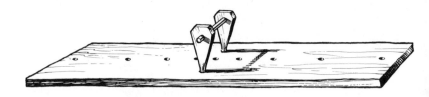

Figure 1. A shadow-clock typical of the type used by the Babylonians and Egyptians circa 1000 B.C. The board was placed on the ground in an east-west direction, and the shadow of the horizontal bar indicated the time marked by the holes.

the bottom, and as the water level fell a reading was taken from markers on the inside wall.

Water-clocks continued to be used for a very long time and Fig. 2 shows a sophisticated design that was in use in Rome and Egypt about 500 B.C. The principle of operation serves to illustrate the progress made.

Water was allowed to drip into a cylinder containing a float. As the water level rose the float lifted a toothed rack that was geared to a wheel which in turn was caused to rotate. Secured to the wheel was a pointer that moved round a circular dial graduated in twenty-four equal divisions. When the cylinder was full of water and the float had reached the top, the cylinder had to be emptied and the cycle was re-started. Provided the device was kept supplied with water it would continue to function and readings were always available.

Another form of water-clock which was in use in England during the seventeenth century, is shown in Fig. 3. It consisted of two wooden uprights bridged at the top from which was suspended, by two lengths of string, an enclosed metal drum that rotated on a central spindle. Fig. 4 shows a cross section of the drum from which it will be seen that a number of baffles was secured to the inner wall.

The spindle was rotated by hand which caused the string to be wound onto each end of the spindle thereby lifting the drum to the top.

Under normal circumstances the force of gravity would

10

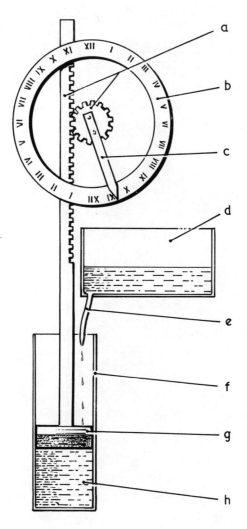

Figure 2. A clepsydra or water-clock used in Rome and Egypt circa 500 B.C.

(a) rack and pinion	(e) controlled drip feed
(b) 24 hour scale	(f) cylinder
(c) pointer	(g) float
(d) water reservoir	(h) water

11

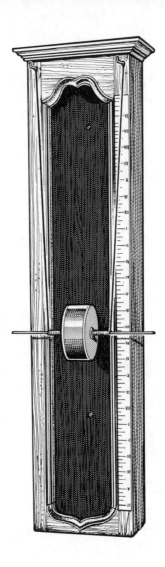

Figure 3. A 17th century English water-clock. Water was contained in the drum which was fitted with tangential baffles allowing the drum to descend slowly from two cords. The spindle indicated the time marked on the scale.

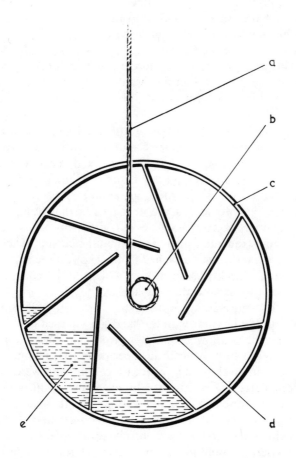

Figure 4. A cross-section of the drum shown in Figure 3.
(a) cord   (b) spindle   (c) drum   (d) baffle   (e) water

cause the drum to fall rapidly and it would spin under the influence of the string. This was prevented by the addition of a small quantity of water which rested in the bottom of the drum and acted as a stabilizer. Small holes in the baffles allowed the water to leak into the adjoining compartments which moved the center of gravity to one side causing the drum to rotate slowly and unwind itself from the string.

This process continued and the drum descended to the bottom of the stand at a uniform rate during which time the hour was read from the graduated wooden frame using the spindle as the indicator.

Candles and oil lamps were also used to measure and indicate the passing of time. Candles were made, possibly of beeswax or tallow, which were marked down the side in hours, half-hours and quarter-hours depending on the size of the candles; as one burned out another was lit.

Oil lamps provided a useful means of indicating the time during hours of darkness. The oil container was made of glass and had a graduated strip of metal on the outside. The base of the oil container was attached to one end of a rectangular tray in which a wick was positioned. Oil from the container was allowed to leak into the tray and as the wick burned the oil level fell and readings were taken from the graduated scale.

We are all familiar with the sand-glasses used as egg timers where sand is allowed to trickle from one glass bulb into a similar glass bulb beneath in a period of four minutes. Sand-glasses date back to the fourteenth century and were made in different sizes to function for fifteen minutes, thirty minutes, one hour and four hours, and were frequently made in sets of four and contained in a frame of wood or metal. They are sometimes referred to as hour-glasses.

At one time sand-glasses were used at sea. It is customary on board ship to divide the twenty-four hours of a day into five watches of four hours, and two watches of two hours. The cycle commences at 12:00 o'clock noon and the ship's bell is rung eight times and the afternoon watch begins. At 12:30 p.m. the bell is rung once; at 1:00 p.m. the bell is rung twice. At 1:30 p.m. it is rung three times, at 2:00 p.m. four times and so on until the afternoon watch ends at 4:00 p.m. when the bell is rung eight times.

From 4:00 p.m. to 6:00 p.m. is the first dog watch and the bell is rung 1, 2, 3 and 4, and from 6:00 p.m. to 8:00 p.m. is the second dog watch when the bell is rung 1, 2, 3 and 8.

The middle watch commences at 8:00 p.m. and finishes at midnight with half-hourly bells ringing 1 to 8 as before. Then the night watch takes over until 4:00 a.m., again with half-hourly bells, followed by the morning watch that remains on duty until 8:00 a.m., at which time the forenoon watch takes over until midday and thereby completes the twenty-four hour cycle.

Sand-glasses were used in the Royal Navy for measuring these thirty-minute periods and this practice continued until the reign of Queen Victoria before it was finally abolished in favor of mechanical nautical clocks.

It was once the practice to use sand-glasses in churches. They were kept in the pulpit so that the clergyman could time his sermon. There is a story of one such reverend gentleman who, having placed his sand-glass in full view of the congregation, preached about the sins of drink at such length that the sand ran out before he had finished. Quickly reaching for the instrument he turned it over and said, "Brethren, we'll have another glass."

In England sundials were popular well into the seventeenth century. During the fifteenth and sixteenth centuries many were scratched in the walls facing the sun of public buildings and churches, and a horizontal hole was bored into which the gnomon was hammered. These were vertical sundials. Others consisted of a slate or brass plate, with the hour marks scratched or engraved, placed horizontally on the top of a stone or brick pedestal in a public place or private garden. Portable sundials that could be carried on the person were in regular use; many examples can still be seen in museums.

Sometimes horizontal sundial plates with gnomons find their way to auctions and antique shops, and one might consider purchasing the plate for use at home in the garden. To make a pedestal is not difficult for the handyman but for the

15

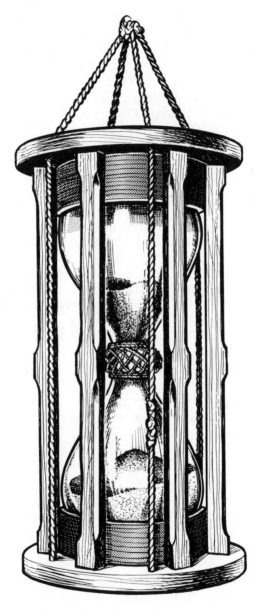

Figure 5. A ship's 4 hour sand-glass.

16

Figure 6. The plate and gnomon of a horizontal sundial.

sundial to function correctly the plate must have been marked
for the latitude in which it is to be used.

There are other examples in museums of man's early attempts to measure the passing of time, but sundials and water-
clocks appear to have been the most popular.

CHAPTER 2
Medieval Clocks

DURING the Middle Ages most churches and monasteries had a bell which was tolled by hand every hour using a sundial or sand-glass as the time indicator. Monks were summoned to prayer in this way, and people in the towns and those working in the fields regulated their days by the sound of the bell. There was a great need for a mechanical clock.

It is not known when and where the first mechanical clock was built, but records show that there were weight-driven striking clocks in abbeys, cathedrals and churches in England from about 1280. Among the earliest known large public clocks are those of St. Paul's Cathedral, London, 1286 - Canterbury Cathedral, England, 1292 - Exeter Cathedral, England, 1300 - Milan Cathedral, Italy, 1335 - Salisbury Cathedral, England, 1386 - Rouen Cathedral, France, 1389 - Wells Cathedral, England, 1392. Of these, only Salisbury, Rouen and Wells have been preserved. That of Salisbury can be seen in the nave of the Cathedral, and the Wells clock is on view in the Science Museum, London.

During the latter half of the fourteenth century and throughout the fifteenth century, clocks appeared in Europe and Britain, but almost all were installed in buildings of worship. They were made of iron and each piece was heated in an open forge and hand-beaten to shape on an anvil by a blacksmith. Parts that required more accurate shaping were

18

Figure 7. A 15th century English wrought iron turret clock which was extensively modified near the end of the 17th century. The original foliot escapement has been replaced by a pendulum and verge escapement. Crown Copyright. Science Museum. London.

Figure 8. Dover Castle clock, England, circa 1600. One of the few remaining turret clocks controlled by a foliot balance. The weighted bar completes a double swing in approximately 8 seconds which allows the main wheel to rotate once each hour. The clock was removed from Dover Castle in 1872. Crown Copyright. Science Museum. London.

20

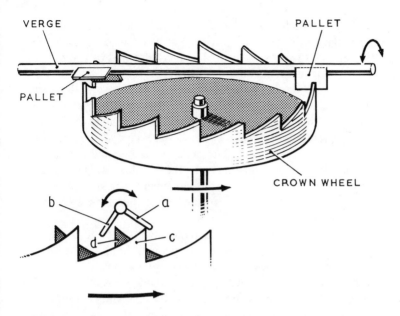

Figure 9. Verge and crown wheel escapement.

finished by filing. When the clocks were assembled they took the form of an open box frame measuring a few feet across. The assembly was usually held together by iron wedges or pins.

It took a long time to make one of these clocks, in some instances, as much as five years, consequently they were costly to produce. Only the wealthy could afford them and so it was inevitable that they first appeared in cathedrals, monasteries and large churches. They were positioned high from the ground because of the amount of fall required by the driving weights and so the obvious place was in the towers. It was for this reason they became known as turret clocks.

The rate at which these clocks were allowed to run down was controlled by a verge escapement and foliot balance, Fig. 9. The escapement consisted of a crown wheel and a verge. The crown wheel was cylindrical with triangular-shaped teeth cut at one end. The verge was an iron rod or piece of wire ac-

21

cording to whether it was a turret clock or domestic clock. On the verge were two pallets spaced at a distance equal to the diameter of the crown wheel. The angle formed by the pallets was a little over one hundred degrees.

The verge was mounted centrally across the mouth of the crown wheel and on one end of the verge was secured a foliot balance. This was a metal bar with a weight at each end which supplied the mass balance necessary to control the speed of the escapement. The ends of the bar had a series of notches to provide adjustment for the weights. By moving the weights outward the rate of the movement was slowed down, and by moving them closer to the center the clock was made to go faster.

The downward pull of the driving weight tried to drive the train of gears but the verge escapement held the train in check. When a crown wheel tooth met a pallet the tooth pushed the pallet forward and clear, and the tooth escaped. At this moment the tooth diametrically opposite encountered the other pallet and the sequence of movement was repeated.

When a pallet was moved by the crown wheel the foliot balance was swung in a semi-rotary direction, and when the other pallet made contact with a tooth the inertia in the balance gave recoil to the crown wheel.

In Fig. 9 tooth (c) is pushing pallet (a) causing the verge to turn counterclockwise. When tooth (c) escapes, the crown wheel continues to rotate until tooth (d) is halted by pallet (b), but the verge still retains some of its mass balance impetus and it pushes against tooth (d) causing the crown wheel to recoil.

The power of the driving weight then takes over and tooth (d) pushes against pallet (b) causing the verge to turn in a clockwise direction. When tooth (d) escapes from pallet (b) the cycle of movement is repeated, and each time a tooth escapes, the crown wheel turns and then recoils, and meanwhile the verge and the foliot are being turned in alternate directions.

This was not a good method of control. The clocks were very unreliable and had to be checked frequently against a

22

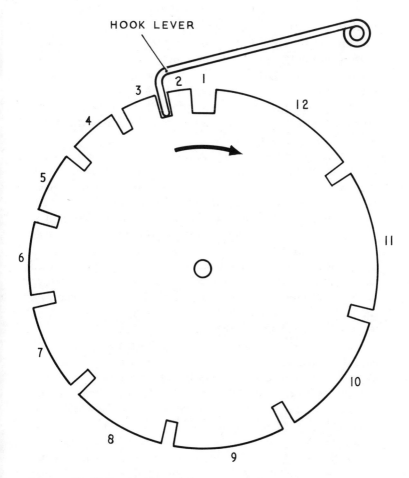

Figure 10. Strike locking plate.

sundial.

Most early turret clocks functioned more or less on this principle, but their means of indicating time varied. Some clocks had dials but did not necessarily have the ability to strike, while other clocks with a strike train may or may not have had dials.

The striking mechanism was called the locking plate

system. It consisted of a hook lever and a locking lever, both of which were secured to the same arbor, and a flat metal disc with eleven notches cut in its periphery which was the locking plate, Fig. 10. The hook lever was bent at its outer end and the hook so formed rested in one of the notches of the locking plate. The locking lever was positioned in the path of a pin fixed to a fast moving strike train wheel by which means the strike train was held at rest.

The mechanism was set in motion by a pin fitted in the rim of the time train wheel that rotated once in every hour. Shortly before the clock was due to strike, this pin made contact with the hook lever lifting it out of the notch in the locking plate. The locking lever was raised at the same time and as soon as it was clear of the arresting pin the strike train was set in motion and the locking plate slowly rotated.

The hammer was actuated by a series of pins spaced equidistant around the edge of either the strike barrel, or one of the wheels in the strike train known as the pin wheel. As the barrel rotated, each pin in turn raised the hammer, and when the pin had passed, the hammer fell and struck the bell.

With each blow of the hammer the hook lever was raised and then allowed to fall back onto the locking plate, but because the locking plate was rotating, the notch would pass beyond the line of the hook lever which would then fall onto the edge of the locking plate between the notches. This sequence of movement continued and the hammer went on striking until the next notch in the locking plate came into line with the hook lever which allowed the hook to drop into the notch. In doing so the locking lever fell back to its former position and the arresting pin was caught and the strike mechanism was brought to rest.

The distance between each pair of notches in the locking plate had to be progressively greater to allow an extra strike for each successive hour up to twelve. The exception was when the clock struck one. In this instance the hook lever was raised, the hammer struck, and the hook lever fell back into the same notch.

The number of blows struck by the hammer was progressive

Figure 11. A 16th century German weight-driven iron chamber
clock with foliot balance. Crown Copyright. Science Museum.
London.

with each release of the strike train and it was not possible for any strike to be repeated.

If the strike weight was allowed to run down and touch the bottom through lack of winding the strike mechanism became inoperative, and if the time train continued to function during this period the hands would become out of coincidence with the locking plate once the twelve o'clock position had been passed. To prevent this from happening both weights had to be kept wound.

When resetting the hand it was necessary that the clock be allowed to strike fully when each hour position was reached. If the hand was moved too quickly and taken beyond the strike position, then the locking plate and the hand became out of coincidence.

Whenever it was necessary to restore the correct relationship between hand and locking plate, the hook lever had to be raised manually and then released to allow the strike mechanism to function through its normal cycle. This process was repeated until the hour struck was coincident with the position of the hand.

It was considered that the possession of a turret clock added to the prestige of a town but because of the high cost a demand arose for a much smaller version that would be less costly. Towards the end of the fourteenth century, such was their growing popularity that smaller clocks began to appear in castles, public buildings and small churches.

Historic records indicate that during the Middle Ages there were no blacksmiths in Britain capable of making a clock. Whenever a clock was required to be made the workman had to be brought from Europe, usually France or Germany.

The manufacture of turret clocks continued. Then, early in the sixteenth century, there was a demand from wealthy families for small clocks that could be used in chamber rooms. The clock parts were fashioned from iron but they were too small to be shaped on an anvil. They had to be filed, and so the work was carried out mostly by locksmiths.

The majority of these new clocks, which became known as chamber clocks, were made in Germany, France and Italy. In appearance they were like miniature turret clocks with a bell on top. An extra wheel was added to the train to reduce the rate of fall of the weights, and the clock was either placed on a shelf or hung on a chamber wall. The making of these clocks in Europe continued well into the seventeenth century during which time little or no attempt was made to alter their Gothic appearance.

CHAPTER 3

Early Spring-Driven Clocks

THERE is documentary evidence to show that spring-driven clocks were probably in use during the late fifteenth century but the earliest known spring-driven clock was made by Jacob Zech of Prague in 1525. It was a circular drum and had a horizontal dial.

In those early days facilities for making steel were limited and, of the little that was produced, most of it was poor quality. After being bent, the metal either snapped or failed to return to its original shape. Many attempts had to be made before a piece of steel was produced that would temper under heat treatment.

It then became apparent that a coiled spring, when fully wound, exerts a greater force than when it is partially wound, a characteristic that was in conflict with a verge escapement, and so disastrous timekeeping was the result.

Then came two inventions, both designed to compensate for this loss of energy. They were the stackfreed that was used by clockmakers in Germany up to about 1620, and the fusee that was generally adopted by other European countries.

The Stackfreed. Fig. 12

Secured to the barrel arbor was a small wheel that was

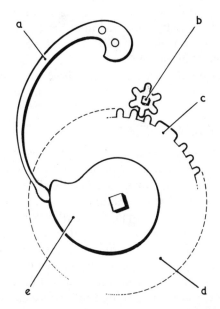

Figure 12. The Stackfreed. A German invention to compensate for the progressive loss of energy experienced in a train when a spring unwound. Used in Germany up to the early 17th century. The drawing shows the stackfreed in the fully wound position.

  (a) spring arm
  (b) barrel arbor (winding end)
  (c) winding stop
  (d) cam wheel
  (e) cam

geared to a large cam wheel on which was secured a cam. Bearing against the edge of the cam was a flat spring which was pushed outward by the rotating action of the cam when the spring was wound. A mechanical stop checked further rotation of the cam when the highest point of the cam lobe reached the flat spring.

When the clock movement was set in motion the tension of the flat spring bearing against the edge of the cam created sufficient friction to slow down the effect of the mainspring until it reached a point when the mainspring was sufficiently un-wound to be incapable of maintaining the required power. At this stage there was little resistance left between the flat spring and the cam and the reverse effect took place in that the tension of the flat spring assisted the cam in rotating and thereby compensated for the lack of energy in the mainspring.

The Fusee, Fig. 13

It was long thought that the fusee was invented by Jacob Zech, but more recently it has been found that a drawing of a fusee appears in a notebook that belonged to Leonardo da Vinci in the late fifteenth century.

The early fusee was a long tapered pulley with a continuous groove cut in a spiral which extended from end to end. Attached to the large end of the fusee was a driving wheel, and to the small end was a squared arbor to receive a winding key.

The spring was coiled inside a cylindrical drum which was positioned next to the fusee so that its axis was parallel to the axis of the fusee. Around the cylinder was wound a gut line, the free end of which was attached to the fusee at its largest diameter.

In this condition the spring was run down. When the key turned the fusee the gut was pulled from the drum, causing the drum to rotate, and the gut was wound onto the fusee in the spiral groove. When the drum rotated it carried with it the outer end of the coil spring; because the inner end was anchored to the stationary center arbor the rotating action of the drum caused the spring to be wound and put in tension. This process continued until the spring was fully coiled. By this time almost all the gut had been transferred to the fusee.

When tension on the winding key was removed the force of the fully coiled spring pulled on the gut which acted on the smallest diameter of the fusee causing the driving wheel to rotate. As the spring uncoiled and the pull on the gut became less, the diameter of the fusee being acted upon became progressively larger giving greater leverage. This method of compensation resulted in the driving wheel being rotated at a

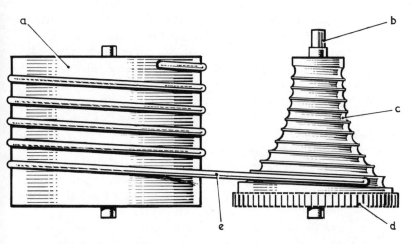

Figure 13. The Fusee. Like the stackfreed, this was designed to compensate for loss of spring energy, but whereas the stackfreed was generally confined to Germany, the fusee was adopted by other European countries. It has remained popular and is today used in many regulator clocks and other precise timepieces. The drawing shows the fusee and spring barrel in the unwound position.
  (a) spring drum
  (b) squared winding arbor
  (c) fusee
  (d) great wheel
  (e) gut line or chain

rate more regular than had previously been achieved.

The fusee is in use in marine chronometers even to this day.

These clocks were known as table clocks but apart from the spring and the stackfreed or fusee the basic movement showed very little departure from the iron chamber clocks; they continued to function under the control of a verge and balance wheel escapement. Their first appearance was in Germany, most of them coming from Nuremburg and Augsburg. Production continued well into the seventeenth century during which time it spread across Europe to Italy, France, Holland and Sweden.

Early table clocks were designed with horizontal dials, usually with only an hour hand. The cases were round, square, hexagonal and octagonal, and were made of wood, brass, marble or ivory, sometimes with inlays of gold and silver. The open work of the cases were skillfully filed and the chased work was that of artists. Beautifully designed panels in colored enamel set in elaborate scroll work were frequently used to decorate the sides.

The clockmakers of Nuremburg became famous for their automata. They would arrange for the strike mechanism to give movement to exquisitely fashioned figurines that would dance, drink or strike bells in a series of small jerky movements.

Late in the sixteenth century some quite small table clocks were made with horizontal dials and round cases with hinged lids. These were known as clock-watches and were the precursors of pocket watches.

In the late seventeenth century other table clocks were made with vertical dials and bob pendulums and were known as tower or tabernacle clocks. They were tall and very ornate. The plinth was usually square and supported by cast feet. The movement was totally enclosed, frequently in a case with architectural corner pillars or statuettes, and surmounted by tiered balconies of metal lacework with hand chased spires.

The movements invariably had strike and chime mechanisms and sometimes alarms. Frequently there would be astronomical subsidiary dials that indicated day of the week, date, moon phases and signs of the zodiac.

There were also pillar clocks which consisted of a base that supported a pillar or crucifix, on top of which was a revolving hour band. The movement was enclosed in the base and the drive to the hour band passed upward inside the pillar while on the base were automata in the form of figurines or animals.

Figure 14. An early English striking tabernacle clock signed and dated Michael Nouwen 1598. Height 9 1/4 inches.

Figure 15. Movement of tabernacle clock. See Figure 14.

Figure 16. An Italian 3 train tabernacle clock with silver dials, gilt and ebony casework. Height 23 inches. Circa 1640.

Figure 17. A solid silver German tabernacle clock of one year duration. The entablature is supported by a caryatid at each corner. Height approximately 24 inches. Circa 1650.

Figure 18. A German striking clock. Circa 1660.

37

Figure 19. (Left) A German 12 hour table clock in gilt brass. Maker Jeremias Pfaff. Circa 1680. (Right) A Bavarian table clock with a gilded brass case and engraved copper dial. Maker Josephus Jans. Circa 1700.

(Left)
Figure 20. The open base of Bavarian table clock shown in Figure 19.

(Right)
Figure 21. Top of Bavarian table clock shown in Figure 19.

CHAPTER 4

English Lantern Clocks (1590-1835)

THE skill of European clockmakers working in London was studied and practiced by their English assistants until, late in the sixteenth century, during the reign of Queen Elizabeth I, a new style of clock emerged made by English clockmakers.

The movement was similar in design to that of the European iron chamber clock except that the foliot was replaced by a heavy rimmed balance wheel secured concentrically to the end of the verge by one radial arm. The wheel moved in a semi-rotary fashion until it was arrested by the verge when one of its pallets engaged a tooth of the crown wheel. This caused the wheel to rebound in the opposite direction until it was again arrested, this time by the locking of the other pallet.

Timekeeping was in no way improved by this method of control, and regulation of the movement was possible only by adding or removing lead shot from a tray in the top of the time weight; an increase of weight caused the clock to go faster.

Two weights were used to drive the clock, one for the time train at the front and the other for the strike or alarm train at the rear. Each weight hung from a rope passing over a pulley adjacent to a great wheel and connected to it by a ratchet. In the well of the pulley were spikes to prevent the rope from slipping, and on the other end of the rope was a small weight to keep the rope taut. Looking at the clock from the front the time train weight hung on the left. This was necessary because the great wheel had to turn counterclockwise to allow its pinion to turn the hour wheel clockwise.

This weight, hanging from one side of the movement, would tend to pull the clock out of the vertical position and so the strike weight was hung on the opposite side to effect a balance. This meant that the great wheel and pin wheel assembly of the strike train would rotate in a clockwise direction, and for the pins to operate against the tail of the strike hammer it was found more convenient to place the hammer on the right-hand side. With the two weights hanging one on each side, balance was restored, the clock remained symmetrical, and the weights were given freedom to operate without touching. Winding was necessary about every twelve hours.

After a few years the English clockmakers broke away from the established practice of using iron and they started making their wheels, frames and dials of brass. Two plates were positioned horizontally, one above the other, and were held apart by four turned corner pillars to which were screwed turned feet at the bottom and turned finials at the top. The wheel trains were planted between vertical bars that were tongued top and bottom between the plates. As with chamber clocks the alarm or strike bell was mounted on the top, and the dial was fitted with one robust hour hand. Around the inner edge of the chapter ring the dials were marked in hours which were sub-divided into quarter-hours to increase the accuracy of reading the time. These new clocks were very popular and they became known as lantern clocks, sometimes referred to as bedpost or birdcage clocks.

The strike mechanism was controlled by the locking plate method, the principle of which has seen little change since the medieval turret clocks. The earliest lantern clocks had their locking plates behind the backplates and these are referred to as outside locking plates. The later clocks were made with the locking plates in front of the backplates and these are known as inside locking plates. Almost all lantern clocks struck each hour but a few were designed to strike each quarter-hour on smaller bells situated beneath the hour bell.

Some lantern clocks had alarm mechanisms and they were fitted with a small circular dial in the center of the main dial and were engraved with Arabic numerals to mark the hour positions.

Secured to the back of the alarm disc was a friction spring that pressed against the hour wheel and caused the hour wheel and alarm disc to rotate as one. Fixed to the friction spring behind the numeral 6 was a pin, Fig. 22.

To set the alarm the disc was turned by hand, thereby overcoming the frictional resistance of the spring, until the time required was positioned beneath the short arm of the hour hand. Providing there were less than twelve hours before the alarm was required the weight was then pulled to the top.

The hour wheel, friction spring, alarm disc and hour hand would rotate together and at the selected time the pin of the friction spring would have reached the top of its travel in which position it would push to one side the alarm operating lever. The rear end of this lever would rotate clear of the alarm arrester pin, allowing the weight to fall and causing the crown wheel and verge to oscillate rapidly. Attached to the upper end of the verge was a hammer head which operated against the inner walls of the hour bell and sounded the alarm for as long as it took the weight to reach the bottom.

Clockmakers then turned their attention to enclosing the movements in cases of brass. A plate was fitted to the back, doors were hung at the sides, and cast frets were mounted above the doors and over the dial partially obscuring the bell. There were many designs of frets of which the Tudor rose, coats-of-arms, lion and unicorn rampant, crossed dolphins, fleur-de-lis, scrolls surmounted by a crown, and entwined oak leaves were but a few. These frets were cast and then filed with great care.

The Roman numerals, or chapters as they are called, and the chapter ring on the dials were engraved and the centers of the dials were chased with elaborate scrolled designs. Some of

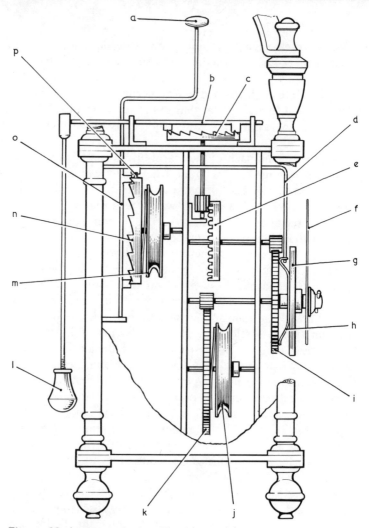

Figure 22. Lantern clock with alarm.

(a) alarm hammer
(b) time verge
(c) time crown wheel
(d) alarm operating lever
(e) contrate wheel
(f) hour hand
(g) alarm setting disc
(h) friction spring
(i) hour wheel
(j) time pulley
(k) great wheel
(l) half seconds bob pendulum
(m) alarm pulley
(n) alarm crown wheel
(o) alarm verge
(p) alarm arrester pin

42

the chapter rings were silvered and it was usual to fill the chapters with black wax.

Until about 1650 the majority of lantern clocks had round dials, the diameters of which were a little more than the width of the clocks. The chapter rings were about three-quarters of an inch in width and the quarter-hour markings were small. Then, during the time of Oliver Cromwell, some clocks had larger dials with wider chapter rings and correspondingly larger chapters. These dials protruded beyond the sides of the clock case and were sometimes referred to as sheep's-heads.

It was fashionable for a clockmaker to inscribe his name, and frequently that of the town in which the clock was made, on the front of the clock. The most usual place was at the base of the fret immediately above the dial but often the inscription was made on the dial itself, sometimes in Latin, e.g. Edmund Massey Londini fecit (made in London).

At the rear of the top plate was a fixed stirrup with which to hang the clock against a beam or on a wall, and behind each rear foot was a spur to project the base of the clock forward into a vertical position to allow the frame to sit squarely with the ropes. Other lantern clocks were made without these fittings if it was intended the clock should stand on a shelf. A hole would be cut in the shelf through which the ropes would hang.

The early lantern clocks were costly and consequently most of them found their way into royal palaces, noblemen's castles, and the homes of wealthy families. Their popularity grew and English clockmakers continued to make them, but little was done to improve timekeeping until the second half of the seventeenth century, during the reign of Charles II, when lantern clocks underwent a number of changes.

In the year 1581 Galileo, the Italian astronomer, became aware of a phenomenon when watching a lamp swinging from a long chain in Pisa cathedral. He noticed that the time taken for a pendulum to complete a swing was always the same regardless of the angle of swing; it swung slowly through a narrow angle and fast through a wide angle. He also found that by increasing the length of the pendulum the time taken to complete a swing was increased and when the length was reduced, the reverse took place.

In 1657 Christiaan Huygens, the Dutch scientist and astronomer, applied these discoveries to a clock. There was in The Hague a very skillful clockmaker, Saloman Coster, who was asked by Huygens to make a movement with a verge escapement incorporating a pendulum. The result was an amazing improvement and for the first time in the history of horology a mechanical device had been made that was

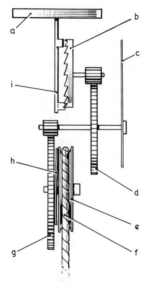

Figure 23. Lantern clock with balance wheel before conversion
(a) balance wheel
(b) crown wheel
(c) hour hand
(d) hour wheel
(e) pulley
(f) rope
(g) great wheel
(h) flat spring click
(i) verge

capable of giving near accurate timekeeping.

Huygens commissioned Coster to make clocks for him incorporating the pendulum. The two men worked together, the one designing and the other producing; together they turned out some excellent pieces of workmanship that were accurate to within a few minutes per day.

In London at this time there lived a family of clockmakers of Dutch descent whose name was Fromanteel. When he heard of Huygens' pendulum clock, John Fromanteel went to Holland to work for Coster and to study the new principle of timekeeping. When he returned to London the Fromanteel family immediately turned its attention to the manufacture of pendulum clocks. Other clockmakers followed their lead and then came a demand to convert existing lantern clocks to pendulum control. This new type of movement was an immediate success and ultimately many hundreds of lantern clocks had their original balance wheels with vertical crown wheels and verge escapements removed and a bob pendulum with horizontal crown wheel and verge escapement fitted. Almost all of these clocks ran for thirty hours between windings, Figs. 23 and 24.

For the first time clocks began to appear with minute hands fitted; such was the faith that clockmakers had in the improved timekeeping of Huygens' pendulum. This necessitated the dial being marked with minute divisions and this was done by producing a minute ring around the outer edge of the chapter ring. A clock that was originally made with only an hour hand and was subsequently modified to include a minute hand can usually be recognized by the absence of the minute ring on the dial. New dials that were engraved with a minute ring still retained the hour ring with the quarter-hour divisions.

News of the pendulum spread across Europe. Surprisingly, however, the German, Italian and Dutch clockmakers continued for another two centuries making clocks in the style of the earlier iron chamber clocks. English lantern clocks had a style of their own. They were better proportioned and better finished and it was not long before England enjoyed an un-

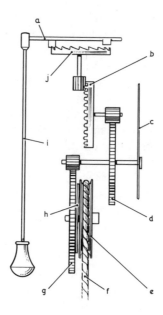

Figure 24. Lantern clock with pendulum after conversion.
(a) verge
(b) contrate wheel
(c) hour hand
(d) hour wheel
(e) pulley
(f) rope
(g) great wheel
(h) flat spring click
(i) half seconds bob pendulum
(j) crown wheel

challenged lead in the field of horology.

The design of the verge escapement was such that a pendulum had to swing through an arc of approximately fifty degrees which necessitated using a short pendulum. A length of about ten inches was convenient because a pendulum of that length was able to swing from one side to the other in a half-second. It became known as a bob pendulum. The time taken for any pendulum to swing from one side to the other is

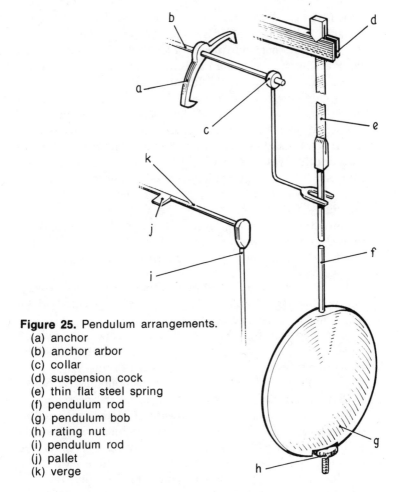

Figure 25. Pendulum arrangements.
  (a) anchor
  (b) anchor arbor
  (c) collar
  (d) suspension cock
  (e) thin flat steel spring
  (f) pendulum rod
  (g) pendulum bob
  (h) rating nut
  (i) pendulum rod
  (j) pallet
  (k) verge

referred to as its rating. A bob pendulum is a half-seconds pendulum.

If the length of a pendulum is increased the effect is to increase the time of swing and it was found that a pendulum of thirty-nine inches took one second. While this was more convenient than a half-seconds pendulum, it was impractical to use because the bottom of the pendulum would have to sweep a distance of nearly three feet.

It had also been discovered that a pendulum swinging through a wide arc could be subjected to a greater time error due to variation of arc than would be the case with a pendulum swinging through a narrow arc. The need then was for an escapement that would function with a long pendulum swinging through a narrow arc. This was accomplished in 1671 by the introduction of the anchor escapement.

We have seen that the early clocks had two weights, one for the time train and one for the strike train, and that each great wheel pulley was fitted with a ratchet. Looking at the clock from the front the time pulley rotated counterclockwise, the strike pulley turned clockwise, and the hammer was fitted on the right-hand side of the movement.

The action of winding caused the great wheels to rotate in reverse and the power of the weights was removed from the trains. When this happened to the time train the movement stopped.

Huygens overcame this problem about 1671 by using only one driving weight and a continuous rope, a method which was known as the endless rope.

As will be seen from Fig. 26, an endless rope is used which passes over the time pulley and over the strike pulley. Hanging from one end of the loop is the driving weight and from the other end is a small weight that supplies sufficient tension to prevent the rope from slipping in the pulleys.

When the rope is pulled downward at A, the strike pulley rotates under the influence of a ratchet and the driving weight is lifted. During this process the downward force of the driving weight continues to be felt by the time pulley and thereby provides continuity of power to the time train.

Between winds the effective driving weight is the difference between the two weights and this difference is imposed on the two pulleys equally. This had the advantage of being able to use one weight to drive both trains whereas two weights had hitherto been necessary.

Unlike the earlier arrangement both pulleys had to rotate in the same direction and, because it was necessary for the time great wheel to retain its counterclockwise rotation, it

48

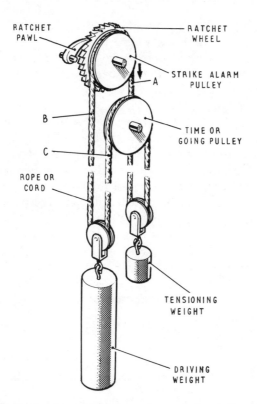

RATCHET PAWL

RATCHET WHEEL

STRIKE ALARM PULLEY

A

B

TIME OR GOING PULLEY

C

ROPE OR CORD

TENSIONING WEIGHT

DRIVING WEIGHT

Figure 26. Huygen's endless rope. An early form of maintaining power. Designed to prevent the clock from stopping when power was removed from the time train during winding.

was the strike great wheel that had to be changed. The pins in the strike great wheel were now attacking the tail of the hammer from the wrong side and so the hammer was moved to the left-hand side of the movement.

It was found that the spikes of the pulleys cut into the ropes and caused fraying and a few years later chains and toothed pulleys were introduced.

This method of providing maintaining power was successful and the principle is used even today in some public clocks.

From a little before the middle of the seventeenth century

until early in the eighteenth century, lantern clocks with pillar frame movements were fitted with square dials and wooden hoods with glass fronts to protect them from dust. It was a sensible idea and they became popularly known as hooded wall clocks.

It is regrettable, but nevertheless a fact, than many old clocks have lost much of their value as antiques due entirely to modifications or conversions to the movement presumably to improve timekeeping. No doubt when the work was done the result was satisfying but an old clock in its original form is worth far more to the collector than one that has undergone alterations. Lantern clocks that have survived the years with their original foliot or balance escapements can command a higher price.

In all their forms lantern clocks were ever popular in Britain, so much so that a few were still being made in the early nineteenth century during the reign of George IV, some two hundred and fifty years after their first appearance.

Figure 27. Lantern clock signed John Greenhill, Maidstone. Balance wheel control. Strike with outside locking plate. Fitted with spurs and stirrup for hanging. Early 17th century.

51

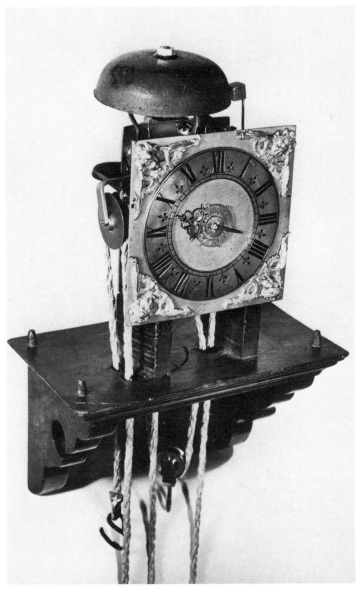

Figure 28. Hooded wall clock signed William Simcox, London. Verge escapement. Alarm. Circa 1682.

Figure 29. Lantern clock signed Phillip Thache, Londini Fecit. Alarm. Circa 1685.

Figure 30. Lantern clock signed Edward Stanton, London. Originally made with a 12-hour movement but converted to 30-hour perhaps only a few years after it was made. Visible evidence of this can be seen by the unusual rope formation and also in the bottom plate. Such a conversion is rare because of difficulties involved in replacing the train and positioning the levers. The majority of these clocks was either scrapped or left in their original state. The 30-hour movement has a verge escapement, bob pendulum, alarm, and a locking plate strike. Circa 1690.

(Left)
Figure 31. A hooded wall clock movement. Verge and crown wheel escapement. Calendar. Hour and quarter strike, outside locking plate.

(Right)
Figure 32. Rear view of hooded wall clock shown in Figure 31.

(Upper Left)
Figure 33. An example of a lantern clock that was converted from balance wheel control to pendulum and back to balance wheel. Height 16 inches. Anonymous. Circa 1692.

(Upper Right)
Figure 34. A lantern clock signed Richard Penny, London. Balance wheel control. Circa 1699.

(Lower Left)
Figure 35. A lantern clock signed Thomas Ford, Buckinghamshire Fecit. Fitted with a minute hand and provided with two key wind holes. Minute divisions on dial. Such clocks are rare. Circa 1724.

(Lower Right)
Figure 36. 30-hour lantern clock movement in a plain oak tallcase. The trunk has a door in the upper half only. The hood has a door at the front and fret panels at the side. The dial has a calendar aperture and engraved ornamentation in the spandrels. Winding is by rope. The dial plate is signed at the bottom Joseph Knibb, Londini, Fecit. Circa 1701.

CHAPTER 5

English Grandfather Clocks (1659-1800)

GRANDFATHER clocks first appeared in 1659 and bracket clocks in 1658. Both were controlled by short half-seconds bob pendulums which at that time were a new invention. The major differences in these two types of clocks were in their source of power and in the size and shape of their cases. Grandfather clocks were driven by weights whereas bracket clocks were spring-driven. During the last four decades of the seventeenth century, development of both types of clocks was rapid, and the inventions that were introduced are among the most important contributions made to the advancement of horology. Both types are much sought after by antique dealers and private collectors but the grandfather clock has the greater appeal. No matter whether it graces a stately house, occupies a position of dignity in a public building, or is part of family life in a suburban home, it is looked upon with affection.

During the time that hooded wall clocks with their thirty-hour lantern movements and short bob pendulums were in fashion, some had their ropes and weights protected and hidden from view by being encased in wooden cupboards. This left visible only the dials and hands. The natural progression from this step took place about 1658 when the hood was removed from the wall and secured to the top of the trunk thereby creating a clock case that stood on the floor.

The half-seconds bob pendulum was short, about nine and a half inches long, and required no more width in which to operate than was taken up by the movement. The wooden case had no need to be wider than was required to give freedom of movement to the weights. The result was a case that was up to six feet tall, very slim, and surmounted by a hood that was proportionately too small for the trunk. The design of the cases was plain and simple and it is not surprising they became known as coffin-clocks.

Before the introduction of the grandfather clock the only demand for wood cases was for hooded wall clocks. These were made by local cabinet-makers. After the tall cases were introduced their popularity grew rapidly and many cabinet-makers found themselves fully employed manufacturing cases for grandfather clocks. Thus a new trade of casemaker began.

Like any other trade there were varying degrees of skill among the craftsmen and, as would be expected, only the most highly skilled were employed on top quality work.

Very little is known about these men. It is believed they were self-employed and made cases to order for the clockmakers. Whoever they were they unfortunately remain anonymous for all time while the names of the clockmakers are permanently engraved on the dials for all to see.

Seventeenth Century

The only important clockmaking center in England was London until the end of the seventeenth century. There were a few provincial clockmakers but the quantity of clocks they produced before about 1680 was small and the cases were typical of London's earliest designs.

During this time London produced many highly skilled clockmakers, and by about 1680 they were acclaimed by other countries as being the leading authorities in horology. Probably their greatest and most extravagant patron and admirer was Charles II who is reputed to have been fond of anything mechanical.

Their clocks, identified by the names engraved on the dials, are keenly sought after because the quality of craftsmanship and beauty of design were nearing their peak of perfection. They are regarded with high esteem by antique collectors throughout the world and can command prices between $3,000 and $50,000. Some of the most eminent English clockmakers are listed in Chapter Eleven, and among their names are those who also made watches.

The number of grandfather clocks produced in London during the second half of the seventeenth century was considerable, certainly more than bracket clocks. Unfortunately, many of the early pieces of both types of clock must have perished in The Great Fire of London that devastated the city in September 1666. Of those that did survive, some are now in museums and most, if not all, of the remainder are in private collections.

Long pendulums were in use by 1675 and their introduction had considerable influence over the size, proportion and design of new cases and dials. A new form of strike control was invented in 1676; known as the rack system it was yet another step forward in the development of the plate frame movement.

The introduction of these new ideas, occurring as they did almost at the same time, makes it convenient to divide the first half century of the life of grandfather clocks into two periods.

1659 - 1675

Very shortly after coffin-clocks first appeared, clockmakers began fitting plate frames to their movements similar to those being used in bracket clocks. With this arrangement wheel trains could be placed side by side, instead of one behind the other as with lantern movements. This made it possible to wind up the weights by means of a key inserted through holes in the dial which fitted over the squared ends of the barrel arbors. The introduction of key winding dispensed with the use of ropes and pulleys, and winding was carried out by gut lines wound round drums or barrels.

59

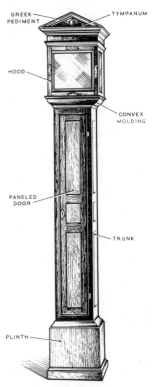

GREEK PEDIMENT

TYMPANUM

HOOD

CONVEX MOLDING

PANELED DOOR

TRUNK

PLINTH

Figure 37. A typical early grandfather clock case. Circa 1660.

In the same period, time trains were fitted with additional wheels to lengthen the running time of the movement from thirty hours to eight days between winds. In some instances time trains were made to run for one month before winding became necessary; but more wheels meant heavier weights to overcome the increase in resistance.

The majority of early grandfather clocks had calendar mechanism and locking plate striking, but chiming or quarter-striking was not usual on the earliest clocks.

In Chapter Four it was said that the action of winding a movement will remove the driving power from a time train and the movement will stop. A number of devices has been used to overcome this problem all of which were known as maintaining power. With the thirty-hour lantern movement the endless rope was used with success but with eight-day movements and their heavier weights the rope method was unsatisfactory.

About 1661 some grandfather clocks were fitted with a different method of maintaining power known as bolt-and-shutter. A cord was hung inside the case, access to which was possible only through the open trunk door. By pulling the cord the maintaining power mechanism was put in operation and at the same time shutters behind the dial plate were moved to one side allowing entry of the winding key. Clocks with bolt-and-shutter are easily recognizable by the presence of shutters behind the winding holes.

Almost all carcasses and panels of the very early cases were made entirely of oak. Some were left in this condition but the majority were veneered with ebony. A few cases were made of

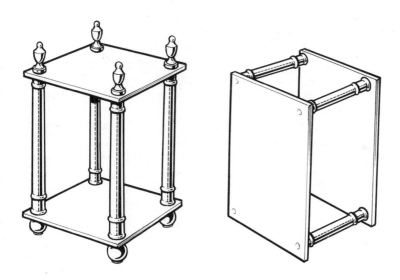

Figure 38. Movement frames. Pillar (left). Plate (right).

pearwood which was stained black and polished to resemble ebony. The front was fitted with a tall square-topped flush-fitting paneled door that had no edge moulding. These doors were usually made with a small panel in the center that carried a lock, and a tall panel above and below. The door gave access to the ropes for winding and at the same time made it possible to see when the weights had reached the top. These pull-up wind clocks are instantly recognized by the absence of holes in the dial through which to insert a key.

The small square hoods were surmounted by a cornice or a Greek pediment which was typical of the architectural styling popular at the time. The sides were fitted with glazed windows through which the movement could be seen. Until about 1669 the height of these side windows was the same as that of the window in front of the dial. Frequently the dial window was flanked either by three-quarter plain, round or fluted Corinthian columns with gilt bases and gilt acanthus leaf capitals, or later by Jacobean style spiral columns which were reminiscent of the James I period. Quarter pillars were sometimes fitted at the rear corners of the hood.

The hoods were made to slide upwards by cutting tongues in the backboard of the case which fitted into grooves in the sides of the hood. When the hands needed to be reset the hood could be raised and held by a catch. Very few lift-up hoods had a door in the front through which the hands could be reached.

Immediately beneath the hood and secured to the trunk was a convex shaped moulding. It is useful to know that this feature applies almost without exception to all seventeenth century English grandfather clocks. It was not until the turn of the century that casemakers began fitting concave mouldings beneath hoods. The point at which the trunk met the base or plinth was frequently covered with a moulding S-shaped in section known as ogee.

An ingenious device was fitted to prevent the unauthorized rising of the hood. Inside the case was a rocking lever, the upper end of which fitted over the bottom rail of the hood, holding it firmly in position. The lower end of the lever rested against the top inside face of the trunk door. When the door was unlocked and opened, the lower end of the lever was free to swing forward and outward and in so doing the upper end swung clear of the hood rail allowing the hood to be raised. When the hood was lowered the trunk door was closed and the lower end of the lever was pushed inward causing the upper end to swing over the rail and relock the hood.

This was the beginning of a style of clock that was to become popular in Europe and North America, but the fashion of the coffin-clock as such lasted little beyond 1669. Later, when the proportions of the case were improved, the reference to coffin-clocks was dropped and in England they were referred to as longcase clocks. When they reached North America they were known by the early colonists as tall clocks. Today, antique dealers and collectors in the United States refer to them as tall-case clocks and so, to prevent confusion of names, we will call them by their colloquial and more modern name of grandfather clocks.

The dial plates were about eight inches square, made of brass, and gilded by a process known as water gilding or mercurial gilding which is the depositing of a film of gold on an inferior metal. To these plates were attached narrow chapter rings held in place by small studs that passed through holes in the dial plate and which were secured at the back by tapered pins tapped into holes in the studs. Chapter rings were usually of silvered brass but in some instances silver was used on high quality clocks.

It might be thought that this was a good opportunity to abolish the use of the hour ring with its quarter-hour divisions, so necessary with the single hand lantern clocks, but the reverse was the case. These quarter-hour markings were retained and appeared on some grandfather clock dials as late as the middle of the eighteenth century.

Against the outer edge of the chapter ring was the minute ring and each fifth division was engraved with an Arabic numeral that appeared inside the ring itself. After being engraved, the chapters, Arabic numerals, rings and divisions were filled with black wax and polished.

The four corner spaces between the curve of the chapter ring and the edge of the dial plate are known as spandrels and it was usual to decorate these spaces with ornaments. Through the years the ornaments themselves have become known as spandrels and it is now the accepted practice to refer to them by this name.

The earliest dial plates were meticulously engraved with a simple winged cherub's head in each of the four corners, and

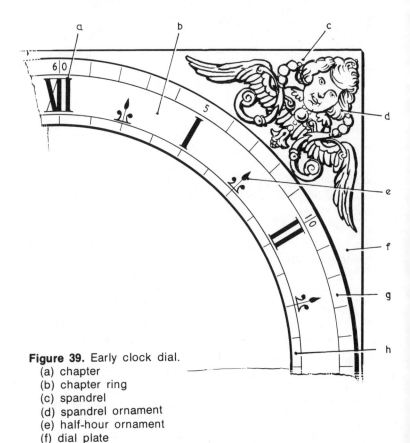

Figure 39. Early clock dial.
(a) chapter
(b) chapter ring
(c) spandrel
(d) spandrel ornament
(e) half-hour ornament
(f) dial plate
(g) minute ring
(h) hour ring

the center of the dial within the hour ring was decorated with an engraved intricate floral design the most popular of which was a tulip pattern.

The engraved spandrels soon gave way to ornaments of similar design that were cast in brass, hand chased and gilded. They were held in position by square-headed screws inserted from the back. These new spandrels stood out in bold relief and the appearance of the dial plates was considerably improved, particularly so in the finest examples of dials when these spandrels were frequently made of silver.

Shortly after the introduction of cast spandrels, London dialmakers began producing dials without the engraved tulip design. Instead, the center was given a matt finish which was produced by uniformly roughening the surface with a metal punch. At about the same time, the appearance of winding holes was improved by fitting them with burnished rings of brass.

Clockmakers engraved their names just above the bottom edge of the dial plate and to read the inscription, or signature as it is sometimes called, it was frequently necessary to raise the hood.

A less popular but nevertheless quite attractive form of decoration was the use of velvet. The cloth was spread over the dial plate and the spandrel ornaments and the chapter ring were placed on top. Sometimes the chapter rings were pierced and their appearance was enhanced by the background of velvet. With such dials the hands were frequently made of hammered brass which further improved the elegance of the dial.

Hands of these early clocks were invariably of simple design. The minute hand was long and slender extending from an S-shaped inner end at the center boss. The length was such that the outer end registered at approximately the center of the minute ring. The hour hand was of a simple spade design which was cut and pierced close to its outer end, and the resultant short point was shaped to terminate at the inner edge of the hour ring. Both hands had square center holes. It was unusual for clocks with half-seconds pendulums to be fit-

Figure 40. Hood tops.
(a) cornice	c. 1670
(b) crested	c. 1675
(c) domed	c. 1680
(d) broken pediment	c. 1690
(e) break-arch	c. 1720
(f) pagoda	c. 1761

66

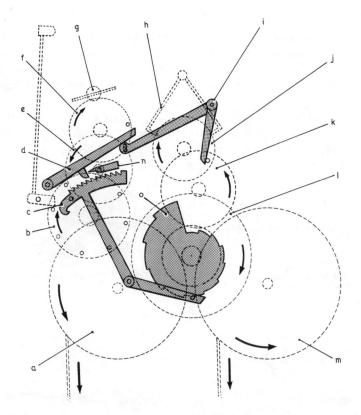

Figure 41. Rack striking work, in 8-day movement, at 6:00 o'clock position.

Strike Train
    (a) strike barrel and
        great wheel
    (b) pin wheel
    (e) pallet wheel
    (f) warning wheel
    (g) governor fly

Strike Mechanism
    (i) lifting piece
    (d) rack hook
    (n) gathering pallet
    (c) rack
    (o) snail (rotates with
        the hour hand)

Time Train
    (m) time barrel and main wheel
    (l) center wheel (hour wheel). Rotates once in 12 hours.
    (k) third wheel (minute wheel). Rotates once in 1 hour.
    (j) escape wheel
    (h) anchor

ted with seconds hands.

In the same way that it had become necessary to institute new trades of casemaker and dialmaker, so it was with the production of hands. The makers cut the hands from steel with skill and precision and they were most particular in that the lengths were correct for the dial to which they were fitted. When shaping was finished the hands were polished and laid in a tray on top of a bed of hot silver sand until they turned blue. This coloring process not only improved their appearance but the oxidizing assisted in retarding the formation of rust.

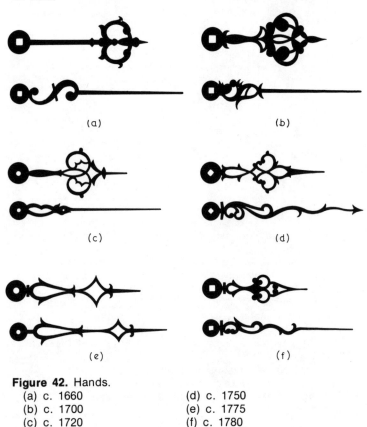

Figure 42. Hands.

(a) c. 1660
(b) c. 1700
(c) c. 1720
(d) c. 1750
(e) c. 1775
(f) c. 1780

To reset a clock, even in the seventeenth century, it was still necessary to refer to sundial readings there being no other method available. It was not until the introduction of the pendulum with its improved timekeeping that it became obvious to clockmakers that something was wrong. At certain times of the year the sundials registered as much as sixteen minutes in advance of the time shown by clocks, whereas at other times of the year the sun was almost as much as sixteen minutes behind.

Astronomers had known for a long time that the time taken for the sun to travel from its meridian on one day to the same position in the sky on the second day varied throughout the year and that the length of each hour was not the same.

A method was needed whereby this solar time could be converted to mean time which was an average over a period of twelve months.

Christiaan Huygens calculated the difference between solar and mean time for each day of the year and then in 1668 John Smith, a London clockmaker and writer of horological matters, began printing equation of time charts from which one could read how many minutes the sundial would indicate in advance or behind mean time for each day. If the sundial indicated 3 p.m. and the equation of time chart showed +8 for the day in question, the clock hands would be set to indicate eight minutes past three o'clock mean time.

The short bob pendulums with their quick action and wide arc of swing continued to be fitted and then came the arrival of the anchor escapement. The credit for this invention is generally attributed to Dr. Robert Hooke but it was William Clement, one of London's eminent clockmakers, who first used the escapement in 1671.

The fitting of this device meant that for the first time long pendulums could function within a narrow arc of swing, but it was not until about 1675 that they appeared in general use.

1676 - 1700

The first of the long pendulums to be fitted were ap-

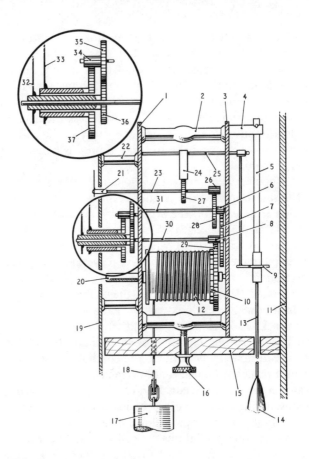

Figure 43. Time train of 8-day movement.

1. front plate
2. plate pillar
3. back plate
4. pendulum cock
5. pendulum spring
6. third wheel pinion
7. center wheel
8. center wheel pinion
9. crutch fork
10. ratchet
11. backboard
12. barrel
13. pendulum rod

14. pendulum bob
15. seat board
16. seat board screw
17. weight
18. line
19. dial
20. barrel arbor
    (winding end)
21. seconds hand
22. dial pillar
23. escape wheel arbor
24. anchor
25. anchor arbor

26. escape wheel pinion
27. escape wheel
28. third wheel
29. main wheel
30. center wheel arbor
31. third wheel arbor
32. minute hand
33. hour hand
34. minute wheel pinion
35. minute wheel
36. cannon pinion
37. hour wheel

70

proximately thirty-nine inches long, this being the length required to produce a rating of one second. Adjustment was carried out by turning a rating nut beneath the bob. These one-seconds pendulums were commonly known as royal pendulums in recognition of the king's patronage.

With this arrangement the timekeeping accuracy was so greatly improved that it was not long before William Clement began experimenting with pendulums of greater length. A few clocks were made that functioned under the control of pendulums sixty-one inches long that had a rating of one and a quarter seconds, but their popularity lasted only until the end of the seventeenth century. These pendulums reached almost to the plinth and cases were made with a door and window in the front of the base. A fine screw adjustment was provided at the mounting of the pendulum to overcome the difficulty of reaching the bob.

With long pendulums the distance travelled by the bob from one side to the other was greater than that of the short bob pendulum. For this reason it became necessary to increase the width of the case. London clockmakers and casemakers alike took this opportunity to break away from earlier designs to produce larger cases of improved proportions which were individually styled and which displayed more elaborate decoration. They had come to realize that the grandfather clock was now as much a piece of furniture as it was a mechanical device and so they began to design their cases more in keeping with furniture styles fashionable at that time.

With the introduction of the one-seconds pendulum the trunk doors were fitted with a round or oval convex glass window, known as a bulls-eye, through which the brass bob of the pendulum could be seen swinging. This was intended to be a visual indication, when no seconds-hand was fitted, as to whether or not the movement was functioning, but the popularity of this window was such that the practice of fitting it continued long after seconds dials had become established.

The art of ebonizing was discontinued in favor of veneered walnut on oak. The oyster pattern also became popular. This

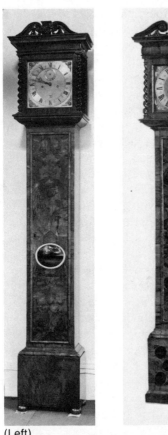

(Left)

Figure 44. 8-day grandfather clock, convex moulding beneath a rising hood. Calendar, strike, bolt-and-shutter, and seconds dial. Center of dial matt, minute numerals inside ring, and simple cast cherub spandrel ornaments. Signed Joseph Knibb, Oxford. Circa 1680.

(Right)

Figure 45. Left hand clock. 8-day oyster case grandfather clock. Strike, bolt-and-shutter, 10 inch dial, calendar and seconds. Height 6 ft. 6 in. Joseph Knibb, Oxford. Circa 1685.

Right hand clock. 8-day walnut grandfather clock. Strike, 10 inch dial, calendar. Case inlaid with marquetry. Height 6 ft. 9 in. Signed Henry Massy, London. Circa 1690.

(Left)

Figure 46. 8-day walnut striking grandfather clock. Marquetry inlaid case. Convex moulding beneath a rising hood. Dial with calendar aperture and minute numerals outside minute ring. Seconds dial, cast spandrel ornaments, and signature in chapter ring. Signed Thomas Clifton, London. Circa 1690.

(Center)

Figure 47. 8-day striking grandfather clock. Walnut case with marquetry panels. Brass and silvered dial, calendar and seconds dial. Late 17th century.

(Right)

Figure 48. 8-day striking grandfather clock. Ebonized carved oak case with rising hood. Calendar, seconds dial and cast cherub spandrel ornaments. Dial with matt center. Minute numerals outside minute ring, and signature in chapter ring. Signed John Stanton, London. Circa 1692.

is a design that is produced by cutting laburnum, and sometimes olive wood, across the grain.

About 1675 cases began to appear decorated with marquetry. The inlay work reflected a strong Dutch influence and at one time it was thought that the cases were made in Holland and exported to London, or that London casemakers sent panels to Holland for completion. More recent thinking is that the cases were made in London and the marquetry was carried out by Dutch immigrant craftsmen.

Popular among the early designs were stars and fans made from triangular shaped pieces of veneer from light and dark woods placed side by side alternately until the pattern was complete, and set against a ground-work of walnut.

By 1680 cases were being decorated with panels covered with intricate floral designs, or patterns dominated by flowers and birds or flowers with vases. The inlays were of boxwood, holly wood, ivory dyed green or in its natural color, and ebony. Some panels were veneered with ebony as the ground-work which served to emphasize the designs and add lustre to the color of the inlays.

Near the end of the seventeenth century the fashion changed from inlay panels in favor of decorating the complete case; this was known as all-over inlay. Marquetry had become an art and the craftsmen responsible for this highly decorative work were in great demand.

The popularity of hoods with architectural styling began to decline at the beginning of this period and about 1685 the pediment had almost disappeared. The flat-topped hood with cornice remained fashionable but makers began to increase the overall height of their cases by fitting a band of fretwork, backed by colored cloth, between the hood and the cornice, and then surmounting the cornice with carved scroll work.

Corinthian style columns had by then almost completely given way to Jacobean spiral columns, and fretwork was occasionally used in place of side windows.

A few years later, about 1680, domed tops were introduced frequently with gilded metal finials in the shape of foliage, balls and flambeaux (flaming torches). The height of cases

Figure 49. Left hand clock. Month striking grandfather clock. Olive wood oyster case with convex moulding beneath hood. Calendar, seconds dial and spade hour hand. Dial 9$\frac{1}{2}$ inches with cast spandrel ornaments and minute numerals inside minute ring. Height 6 ft. 6$\frac{1}{2}$ in. Signature at bottom of dial plate Joseph Knibb, Londini Fecit. Circa 1679.

Right hand clock. Month striking grandfather clock in burr walnut. Hood with fret side panels and plain round columns with gilded capitals. Calendar, seconds dial and bolt-and-shutter. Dial with cast spandrel ornaments, minute numerals outside minute ring. Signature at bottom of dial plate by Thomas Tompion. Clock No. 365. Height 7 ft. 10 in. Circa 1703.

had by then reached about seven feet.

During the following years domed hoods with their finials grew in height until the lift-up hood became unmanageable. Then, about 1685, hoods were made to slide forward so that they could be removed without being raised, and a hinged glazed door was fitted at the front to provide access to the dial.

Many of these hood doors were secured by means of an iron staple and wooden peg. The staple was fixed to the inside of the door in the bottom rail and when the door was closed the staple passed through a slot cut in the base of the hood frame. A wooden peg was then passed through the open trunk door and inserted in the staple from behind. This device continued to be in use until the late eighteenth century.

The Jacobean columns that flanked the hood door became less popular near the end of the seventeenth century and they were replaced by plain round columns which were more slender than the earlier Corinthian style columns.

With the advent of larger hoods the size of dials was increased to ten inches, and the minute numerals were engraved around the outside of the minute ring larger than had previously been possible. This made them more legible. The quarter-hour divisions remained.

The simple spade type hour hand disappeared and the pierced work of the new hour hands was bigger and more decorative.

The introduction of the one-seconds pendulum now made it desirable that seconds hands be fitted. The seconds dials had narrow chapter rings which were marked with sixty divisions for a one-seconds pendulum, and forty-eight divisions for a one and a quarter seconds pendulum, these being the respective number of beats each made in one minute. The hands were long and slender, and at no time during the seventeenth century were they made with tails.

Cases and hoods continued to grow and about 1690 eleven-inch dials were being fitted. These large dials needed bigger spandrel ornaments and the simple cherub design of earlier clocks gave way to new designs; two of the more popular being a woman's head surrounded by an arabesque pattern, and a central crown supported by a cherub on each side.

It was about this time that clockmakers began engraving their names between the chapter ring circles at either side of the Roman numeral VI instead of the bottom edge of the dial plate as in earlier clocks.

Dials continued to grow and by the end of the seventeenth century they had reached twelve inches in size.

In 1676 Dr. Edward Barlow invented a new method of controlling the strike known as rack striking. Thomas Tompion applied the idea to his clocks almost immediately.

The locking plate system allowed the hours to be struck in correct sequence regardless of the position of the hands which meant that if the hands were turned manually, or if the strike train was accidentally released, the hands and the strike would not be correctly related. The mechanism had then to be lifted manually to release the strike, and the process repeated until the strike was once again coincident with the time shown by the hands.

This disadvantage does not exist with the rack system because the strike mechanism is connected to the dial wheels that turn the hands and the one cannot move without the other.

The early racks were fitted between the plates and were known as inside racks, but about 1710 the design changed and the racks were fitted outside the plates.

In 1695 Tompion devised a mechanical means of indicating the equation of time which dispensed with the need of charts. The mechanism was fitted to the top of the movement and it became necessary to extend the clock dial upward to make provision for the equation of time indicator. This new shape took the form of a semi-circle mounted on top of the original square and became known as a break-arch or broken-arch dial. The first of such clocks produced by Tompion was made for William III in 1695.

In the meantime, the popularity of the lantern clock remained and for this reason many provincial makers continued to produce them almost to the end of the eighteenth century. The movements followed the traditional design of placing the strike train behind the time train, and they were controlled by short pendulums with crown wheel and verge escapements, or long pendulums with anchor escapements. Winding was carried out daily by the pull-up method using rope and spiked pulleys or chain and toothed pulleys, and therefore there were no winding holes in the dials. Square brass dials replaced the former round dials but the single hour hand and the engraved hour ring were retained. There were no minute rings on the dials.

To keep pace with fashion, these lantern type clocks were installed in tall plain oak cases. No doubt they were less expensive than their contemporaries, a fact which must have influenced the continued demand. There are still a number of these clocks in circulation, all of which have an antique value; it must not be assumed that they are necessarily seventeenth century.

The locking plate method of strike control as used in lantern clocks was fitted in the earliest grandfather clocks. Quarter-striking and chiming mechanisms did not appear until a few years after the introduction of the plate frame movement.

The first to appear was the ting-tang quarter-striking similar to that which was used in sixteenth century turret clocks and chamber clocks. In addition to the large bell on which the hours were struck, there were two smaller bells of dissimilar pitch for the quarter-hours. At the first quarter the two small bells were struck once and produced the sound described as ting-tang. At the half-hour the bells were struck twice, at the third quarter three times, and lastly on the hour they were struck four times followed immediately by the hour strike.

By 1690 chiming clocks were in regular use. The quantity of bells used varied between clocks, but none had less than four. They had to be small because space was limited but even so they were well cast, when struck they produced clear but quiet rings that had a charm of their own. By varying the quantity and mixing the sizes of the bells the clockmakers were able to produce a variety of simple melodies. The usual

 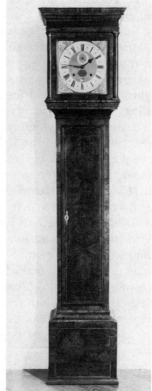

(Left)

Figure 50. 8-day striking grandfather clock. Plain wood case with shaped top to lay-on type door. Hood with paneled sides and plain round columns. Calendar and seconds dial. Cast spandrel ornaments, minute numerals outside minute ring, and signature in chapter ring. Signed Matthew Crockford, London. Circa 1705.

(Right)

Figure 51. 8-day striking grandfather clock. Note the two bells for Roman striking and the unusual Roman numeral IV on the dial. Outside locking plate. Rising hood with flat top and plain round columns. Calendar and seconds dial. Cast spandrel ornaments, minute numerals outside the minute ring, and signed in the center Dan. Quare, London. Clock No. 111. Circa 1706.

method of sounding the quarter-hours was to chime a simple scale, once for the first quarter, twice for the half-hour and three times for the third quarter. The chime that preceded the hour strike was either the simple scale played four times or a little melody.

Some chiming mechanisms had their own wheel train and weight which meant that the dials would be made with three winding holes for time, strike and chime.

The very earliest chiming clocks were fitted with locking plates that controlled the strike and the chime, but in later clocks the strike was controlled by a rack while the locking plate was retained for the chime.

In 1676 Edward Barlow invented a new method of strike control known as rack striking, but it was Thomas Tompion who was the first to use it. From then on Tompion fitted rack striking to all his clocks but not all clockmakers followed his example. It was not until about 1710 that rack striking became the accepted method for grandfather clocks. Locking plates were still being used in some eight-day movements during the eighteenth century and some thirty-hour movements in the nineteenth century. Then, when the grandfather clock became less popular, the locking plate fell into disuse.

The early racks were fitted between the plates of the movement; then about 1710 they were positioned in front of the front plate behind the dial.

Fig. 41 shows a rack strike mechanism about to strike six. Shortly before the hour is due to be struck, the third wheel (k) of the time train has moved round and the pin is pushing against the lower arm of the lifting piece (i). The upper arm of the lifting piece has raised the rack hook (d) clear of the ratchet teeth in rack (c) allowing the rack to swing counterclockwise. The pin in the lower arm of the rack is arrested by snail (o). The snail is a flat plate with a series of twelve progressive cams cut in its periphery, the deepest cam allows the hammer to strike twelve times and the highest cam allows the hammer to function once only.

Until now the strike train has been prevented from moving

by the tail of the gathering pallet (n) resting against the pin in the rack, but when the rack swings away from the gathering pallet, the strike train is released and able to rotate. Further raising of the lifting piece will place the warning piece, fixed in the end of the upper arm, in the path of the oncoming pin in the warning wheel (f) and the strike train will again be arrested. This initial but brief run of the strike train is known as the warning.

Exactly on the hour, the pin in the third wheel (k) will pass and release the lifting piece which will swing counterclockwise taking with it the warning piece away from the pin in the warning wheel (f). The strike train will then be free to run until the strike has been completed.

When the pin wheel (b) rotates, the pins will operate the bell hammer. At the same time, the pallet wheel (e) will rotate carrying with it the gathering pallet (n) which will gather the rack one tooth for each strike of the hammer. When the last tooth has been gathered, the tail of the gathering pallet will again be arrested by the pin in the rack and the strike train will come to rest.

The fly (g) acts as a governor and generally controls the regularity of the hammer blows. The greater the surface area of the fly, and the higher the speed of rotation, the greater will be the air resistance. Such an arrangement will produce slow hammer movements causing the bells to ring with a mature mellow sound.

In an eight-day clock there must be enough energy to operate the hammer about 1250 times, more if the clock strikes between the hours. A clock that will run for twenty-eight days will require power to produce 4368 hammer blows striking hours only. For this to be possible in a weight-driven clock additional gearing must be used to prevent the weight's reaching the bottom of its fall prematurely. A very heavy weight is needed to overcome the resultant increase in resistance. Likewise, in a spring-driven clock, such as a bracket clock, the increase in gearing resistance can be accomplished only by the use of a long and powerful spring.

Joseph Knibb overcame this problem by introducing a

81

system, known as Roman striking, that was controlled by a locking plate and which reduced the number of hammer blows to 60 each day instead of 156. Two bells of different notes were used and were related to the formation of the Roman numerals on the dial. The higher pitched bell was sounded once for numeral I, and the lower pitched bell was struck once for numeral V and twice for numeral X, e.g., II would be high high, VII would be low high high, and IX would be high low low. The four o'clock position on the dial was marked IV instead of the usual IIII. An example of this can be seen in Fig. 52. Clocks with Roman striking are rare and can command a high price.

Figure 52. Dial of Grandfather clock shown in Figure 51.

Towards the end of the seventeenth century, a different form of strike was introduced which was known as Dutch striking. This arrangement involved the use of two bells of different pitch. The hours were struck on the bell with the lower tone, and at the half hours the next hour was struck on the bell with the higher tone. For example, at four o'clock the hammer would strike the low toned bell four times, while

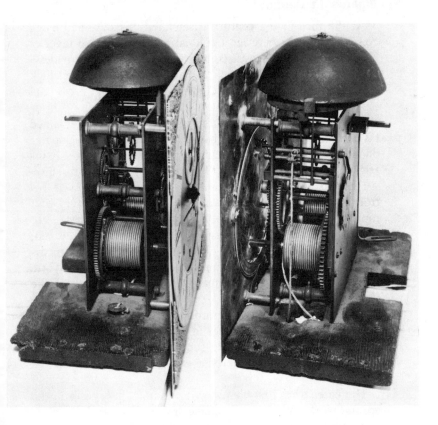

Figures 53 and 54. Side views of Grandfather clock shown in Figure 51.

at half past four the high toned bell would be struck five times. The cycle would start again at five o'clock when the low toned bell would receive five blows from the hammer. At the end of the seventeenth century this method of striking was further developed into what became known as grande sonnerie.

Eighteenth Century

At the turn of the century casemakers discontinued using convex moulding between the hood and the trunk in favor of moulding with a concave section. This substitution provides a good indication as to which of the two centuries the clock belongs. The number of clocks produced by provincial makers was on the increase, and the practice of using oak for the lower priced cases continued. Marquetry remained fashionable in London and by about 1710 the most popular decoration consisted of foliage and other shapes curiously intertwined all over the case. This was known as arabesque.

Lacquer work, or Japanning as it was called, was introduced at the beginning of the eighteenth century and rapidly gained in popularity. The paneled designs were typically Japanese in origin and worked in brilliant blue, red, green and gold against a background of black. The process was lengthy and required considerable patience and artistic skill, both of which are often considered attributes of the Oriental.

The Japanese lacquer-tree produces a dark red transparent juice that appears on the twigs in the form of resin and if this is mixed with a volatile fluid such as alcohol the result is a very fine and glossy lacquer varnish to which coloring can be added.

The cases were first coated with black lacquer to form the ground-work and then successive layers of colored lacquers were applied until the design stood out in bold relief.

The cases were shipped to Japan for the work to be carried out and then sent back to England for the movements to be fitted. This proved to be a very lengthy and costly procedure and clockmakers were obliged to find an alternative method.

Figure 55. This is an unique grandfather clock by Daniel Quare, London. It is the only known clock by him that runs for one year and strikes for one year on each winding. The case is inlaid with turtleshell, pewter and brass, and stands 7ft. 10 in. high. Circa 1715.

Figure 56. 8-day striking grandfather clock. Burr walnut break-arch case. Calendar and seconds dial. Plain round columns with gilt capitals. Signed William Barrow, London. Circa 1720.

86

To reduce the cost, cases were made of soft white wood and black lacquered in England, and only the trunk doors were sent to Japan. This method continued for a few years but there was still the delay in waiting for the return of the doors which in those days of sailing ships meant many months. To overcome this problem, craftsmen in England and Holland began practicing Japanning until their proficiency was such that it became difficult to differentiate between their work and that from the East.

In the same way that the popularity of marquetry passed from paneled designs to all-over patterns so it was with Japanning. All-over lacquer work began to appear about 1730 after which there was a gradual decline in popularity until about 1760 when very little lacquer work was produced.

Today there are very few cases that can display lacquer work in good condition. Heat, damp and sunlight have taken their toll and much of the lacquer has flaked from the ground-work.

About 1720 a new fashion was started, that of decorating the cases with figured or burr walnut. Identical sheets of walnut veneer, selected for their beauty of grain, were alternately reversed and placed side by side to produce symmetrical designs. This method of decoration was immensely popular. Some of the best George II cases were made in this way, but the introduction of walnut marked the beginning of the decline of marquetry work.

Trunk doors with shaped tops began to appear about 1720, among the earliest of which were the break-arch variety. Two and sometimes three ball spires were fitted to the tops of some hoods, further increasing the height of the clocks to between eight and nine feet. Around 1750 the making of lift-up hoods was discontinued in favor of the forward sliding hoods.

From about 1740 to about 1760 the production of grandfather clocks in England was almost non-existent. After this period the production was taken over by provincial clockmakers, particularly in the counties of Yorkshire and Lancashire, who produced many thousands of clocks. Their designs followed the earlier London patterns together with new designs of their own. About 1760 they introduced many variations of the horned or swan-neck design, the carvings of which were part of the main structure of the hood and not an addition to be fixed on the top. Very shortly after, about 1761, the pagoda topped hood appeared. The Oriental characteristics of this design strongly resemble those in the period furniture by Thomas Chippendale and it seems reasonable to assume that the casemakers were prompted by this influence.

After 1760 London clockmakers concentrated on the manufacture of bracket clocks and the only grandfather clocks made were those to special order which usually meant they were to be clocks of high quality.

The introduction of mahogany for the manufacture of cases took place about the time that George III came to the throne in 1760. The first of these woods to be used was Spanish mahogany from the island of San Domingo. The wood was close grained, heavy and dark brown in color. Then came the Cuban mahogany that was lighter in weight and had a wavy grain. This was followed by mahogany from Honduras, frequently referred to as bay wood, which was even lighter in weight and was reddish brown in color. The demand for mahogany continued throughout the eighteenth century but during the closing years the fashion began to decline.

It is known that in the early years of the eighteenth century a few dials were made with an Arabic numeral engraved at each minute division, but such dials are rare.

The early practice of a clockmaker's engraving his name at the bottom of the dial began to disappear and about 1710 signatures appeared in the center of the dial, either above or below the hand bosses. About the same time, seconds hands were given counterpoise by adding tails.

After the appearance of the first equation clock in 1695 by Tompion, other London clockmakers followed his lead. By about 1720 the use of break-arch dials had become generally accepted throughout England, even with clocks that had no equation work. The extra space at the top of the dial was used to accommodate subsidiary dials to indicate chime, strike-silent, and calendar. Quite frequently the maker's name would appear in the arch engraved on a raised and silvered boss.

During the next few years dialmakers discontinued the use of half-hour ornaments and quarter-hour division rings and, by 1725 they had almost disappeared.

By 1730 moon dials began to appear in the break-arch. There were many variations but in general principle these dials consisted of a brass disc with teeth cut in its periphery. Early dials were usually engraved and silvered and because they rotated once for every two lunations, the discs carried two painted moon faces diametrically opposite. Between the two moons were a landscape and a seascape, and around the outside edge was a ring of numbers. As the disc rotated it was viewed through an opening in the main dial arch and a pictorial representation of the moon's phase was apparent together with the age of the moon indicated by a number through a second and smaller aperture.

Center seconds hands and serpentine minute hands with arrow heads were in use by 1750.

Makers of hands had always been meticulous with their cutting, particularly in respect to the accuracy of length, but about 1760 there were signs that attention to this detail was being relaxed. Clocks were produced with hands that extended beyond the hour and minute rings.

It was about this time that brass break-arch dials first appeared with engraved and silvered centers. These remained popular but some fifteen years later there was an increasing demand for cheaper clocks. About 1775, white painted iron dials were fitted to low priced clocks. The numerals were painted black, usually Roman but sometimes Arabic, and the spandrel corners were decorated with floral designs in colored paints. The hands were blued or oil blacked steel but frequently gilded; pierced hands were fitted. At the same time that painted dials appeared, matching hands were introduced. Painted dials are generally not popular among collectors.

The dial arch was invariably filled either with some automata such as a windmill with rotating sails or a rocking ship, or with calendar work or moon work with local high water indication.

At the other end of the cost scale were the expensive clocks of which the very best were usually fitted with one piece silvered brass break-arch dials with engraved chapter rings, numerals, dial centers and spandrels, all of which were filled with black wax and polished. Matching hands were popular.

The variety of designs and shapes of hands in use during the seventeenth and eighteenth centuries is very wide and the task of producing an illustrated catalog is almost impossible. Most makers designed their own hands but there were some universal patterns that can assist in determining the period in which they were made. Examples of these can be seen in Fig. 42, and the annotated year is when it is thought that the type of hand was first introduced. It must be remembered that hands are easy to change and should not be regarded as proof of the age of the movement.

About 1785 brass dials began to appear with dots in the minute ring instead of radial lines, and a few years later this practice found its way to painted iron dials.

Throughout the eighteenth century it was the practice to use solid oak without veneer or other decoration for the cheaper clocks and after about 1760 solid mahogany was also used.

Towards the end of the eighteenth century the elegance of the earlier cases began to disappear. The trunks were wider, hoods were larger, dials had reached fourteen inches, and the general effect was ill-proportioned and unartistic.

Unlike the seventeenth century there were few changes to the movement during the eighteenth century.

About 1710 striking racks were moved from between the plates to a position immediately behind the dial and were known as outside racks.

Bolt-and-shutter maintaining power was in use up to about 1720 after which date it was rarely fitted.

In 1752 England adopted the Gregorian calendar which made existing equation work incorrect. Owners of equation clocks had to have the mechanism altered or allow it to fall into disuse. After 1752 equation work was rarely fitted.

At the beginning of the eighteenth century, chiming clocks were using six, and in some instances as many as eight, bells in a chime. A modified form of Dutch striking was introduced which allowed the chiming of each quarter to be preceded by the previous hour. Thus, if a quarter chime was heard during the night, there was no doubt to which hour the quarter chime referred. This arrangement was known as grande sonnerie and its popularity lasted until about 1730 after which it was rarely fitted.

The development of chiming clocks continued and by about 1770 chiming and musical movements with four trains were being made, and in some instances were fitted with as many as twenty-four bells. With the growth of the movement, larger hoods were needed and so it became necessary to manufacture wider cases.

The playing of a simple scale at each quarter-hour was replaced by the chiming of a short tune or melody. Some clocks chimed immediately before the hour was struck, and afterwards a popular tune of the period would be played. A variation of this arrangement was to play tunes immediately after striking three, six, nine and twelve o'clock, and to chime a scale immediately before striking the remaining hours.

These clocks were invariably fitted with subsidiary dials in the break-arch whereby control of chimes and strikes was possible. A tune selector was fitted. This consisted of a pointer that could be manually turned within its own dial which was engraved with the titles of up to about twelve tunes. When selection was made the chime barrel was moved along its own axis thereby offering a different set of pins to the hammer tails. Other manual controls in the break-arch were engraved Strike-Silent, Chime-Silent, and Music-Silent, all of which provided the owner of the clock with full control of all audible time indications.

Of the many four-quarter chimes in common use the most popular is the Westminister. About 1788, Dr. Crotch, a leading authority on church music, adapted the aria "I know that my Redeemer liveth" from Handel's "Messiah" for use in

Figure 57. 8-day mahogany striking grandfather clock with fluted columns to trunk and hood. Break-arch dial and swan neck pediment top surmounted by turned wood finials. Engraved brass dial with center seconds hand and center calendar hand, with moon phase in the break. Height 8 ft. Signed Ralph Eden, Liverpool. Circa 1770.

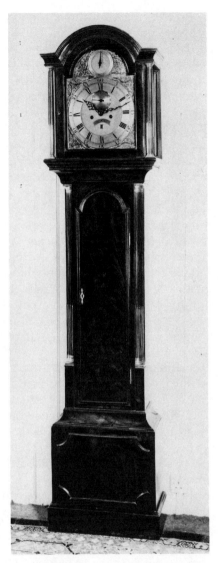

Figure 58. 8-day mahogany striking grandfather clock. Fluted columns to trunk and hood. Calendar, seconds dial, and strike-silent dial in the break-arch. Height 6 ft. 11 in. Signed John Wilson, London. Circa 1780.

the clock of Great St. Mary's Church, Cambridge, England. The chime was subsequently used in the Big Ben clock of the Houses of Parliament, Westminster, London, from which the chime derived its name.

The plate frame movement superseded the earlier lantern type pillar frame movement in 1658 and in general principle the design has been altered little and is still the accepted method for modern clocks.

In the pillar frame the strike train was positioned behind the time train and winding was effected by pulling on ropes. The plate frame did away with this method and allowed the two trains to be positioned side by side. In so doing it became possible to raise the weights by means of a key placed on the front ends of the barrel arbors. This dispensed with the use of ropes and spiked pulleys and allowed gut lines to be employed which were wound directly on to the barrels.

The plate frame consisted of two sturdy brass plates which were held apart by turned brass pillars and the assembly was then used with the plates in the vertical position. Between the plates were the wheels and pinions mounted on their arbors, the ends of which were machined to produce pivots which rotated in holes drilled in the plates.

The size of the frame varied according to the type of movement. For the thirty-hour movement the frame was small, but for movements of greater duration, necessitating the use of more wheels, the frame was proportionately larger. Very big movements, such as those produced during the second half of the eighteenth century, required even bigger hoods. To maintain some kind of acceptable proportion the trunk of the case had to be widened.

The pillars were riveted to the back plate and the opposite ends were reduced in diameter to pass through holes in the front plate, after which they were held in position by the insertion of tapered pins.

Up to about 1725 the majority of movements received considerable attention to the appearance of the pillars and the plates. The pillars were shaped in the lathe and then burnished. Frequently they were decorated with etching, while the plates were carefully cut and given a high polish. During the seventeenth century the number of pillars used was invariably four, although frames with three or six were not uncommon. At the turn of the century clockmakers seemed to have settled to the idea of using four pillars and it is unusual to find an eighteenth century movement with any other quantity.

Until the middle of the eighteenth century almost all frames had their bottom pillars drilled and tapped to receive hand screws that passed upward through the seat board and which when tightened held the movement firmly in position.

The same care was extended to the remaining parts of the movement; the surfaces were polished wherever possible and many were burnished. In high quality work the general finish and appearance of the movement was equalled only by the perfection of the case in which it was fitted.

During the second half of the eighteenth century there was progressively less attention given to the appearance of the movement. Individual parts were inclined not to be polished. Plate pillars were not engraved and they became plain in shape. The bottom pillars ceased to be drilled and tapped to receive seat board screws. Instead, the frame was held to the board by steel hooks that fitted round the pillars and were held in place by nuts and washers beneath the board.

The seat boards were made of thick wood, usually oak. They were supported at each end by the sides of the case trunk, and were cut away to provide clearance for the lines and freedom for the swinging pendulum. If the board is sound, and fits snugly in the case, the weight of the movement plus that of the weights will hold the board in place. In such circumstances the board does not need to be screwed down, but if it is warped or split, or has been rendered unsafe by the activities of wood-worm, then it should be renewed.

The first plate frame movements had a duration of thirty hours, but it was not long before clocks were made to run for eight days between winds by fitting extra wheels. By 1660 month clocks had become established and twelve-month

Figure 59. 8-day striking grandfather clock. Red lacquered case with break-arch, calendar and seconds dial. Signed Charles Hanson, London. Later 18th century.

timepieces were not unknown. The addition of wheels raised the gear ratio and increased the frictional resistance of the train, which necessitated the use of larger weights.

All early plate frame movements were controlled by short half-seconds pendulums until the introduction of the long pendulum with anchor escapement about 1675.

The thirty-hour clocks retained the pull-up wind method and used the endless rope, first with rope and spiked pulleys and later changing to chains and toothed pulleys. The time train was fitted on the left of the movement viewed from the front, and the strike train was on the right.

Plate frame movements of greater duration transmitted the power of the weight to the wheel train by using gut line which was wound on to a barrel. The trains were positioned in reverse order to those of thirty-hour clocks in that the time train was on the right and the strike train on the left.

The wheels of the different trains are shown in the following table. Three-month clocks with a strike train are very rare, and six-month and twelve-month movements were timepieces only; i.e. they had no strike mechanism. Such clocks were usually made to special order.

The minute hand is carried by the third wheel on a thirty-hour clock and by the center wheels of the other clocks. These wheels have to rotate in a clockwise direction and the main wheels must, therefore, rotate in such a direction as to allow this to happen. Allowing for the fact that when winding a clock the main wheel is turned in the opposite direction to normal rotation, we find that the direction of winding is counterclockwise for a month clock and clockwise for all other movements.

The most popular grandfather clocks were those fitted with eight-day movements. Fig. 42 shows the time train in diagrammatic form.

One end of the line is secured to the barrel and the other end passes under the weight pulley and up through a small hole in the seat board, after which it is looped and knotted. If the hole is too large to hold a knot it is usual to tie the line to a small metal bar.

The barrel and the ratchet are secured to the barrel arbor but the main wheel is free to turn about the arbor. On the face of the main wheel is a click which engages the ratchet teeth under pressure from a spring. When the winding key is placed over the barrel arbor and turned in a clockwise direction, the barrel and ratchet rotate and the line is wound on to the barrel. During this operation it is essential that the trunk door be kept open so that the rise of the weight can be watched. If the weight is taken too high and the pulley is allowed to hit the under surface of the seat board, the shock could easily snap the line. The weight would then fall to the bottom causing damage to the case and making it necessary to repair

Duration	Weight	Time Train	Strike Train
30-hour	8 lbs.	Main wheel Third wheel Escape wheel	Great and pin wheel Pallet wheel Warning wheel
		Strike Train	**Time Train**
8-day	12 to 14 lbs.	Great wheel Pin wheel Pallet wheel Warning wheel	Main wheel Center wheel Third wheel Escape wheel
Month	30 lbs. plus	Great wheel Intermediate wheel Pin wheel Pallet wheel Warning wheel	Main wheel Second wheel Center wheel Third wheel Escape wheel
3, 6 and 12 months	100 to 130 lbs.		Main wheel First wheel Second wheel Center wheel Third wheel Escape wheel

the line, if not to renew it completely. When the barrel and ratchet are turned the click rides the ratchet teeth, but when winding stops and the weight tries to turn the barrel and ratchet in the opposite direction, the click spring holds the click into the ratchet and the power is transmitted to the main wheel.

The weights vary in poundage according to the duration of the movement. They were usually made of cast iron, but in high quality clocks lead was frequently used and housed in polished brass tubular containers.

When the weight is in suspension, power is transmitted from the main wheel to the center wheel pinion and then from wheel to pinion in succession until it reaches the escape wheel, the last in the train. The anchor, which is immediately above, is so positioned that its pallets interrupt the path of the escape wheel teeth and prevent the escape wheel from rotating freely.

When the pendulum swings, the anchor is caused to rock, thus releasing one tooth of the escape wheel. When the pendulum swings in the opposite direction another tooth is released. The escape wheel delivers an impulse to the anchor each time a tooth pushes against the face of a pallet and it is this impulse that maintains the swinging motion of the pendulum.

The number of teeth in each wheel and the number of leaves in each pinion govern the gear ratio between each pair of wheels. The main wheel of an eight-day clock fitted with a one-seconds pendulum rotates once in twelve hours, the center wheel once each hour, the third wheel once in seven and a half minutes, and lastly the escape wheel once every minute. The center wheel is used to drive the minute hand while the escape wheel drives the seconds hand. The center wheel also drives the hour hand by means of a group of wheels known as dial wheels which have a gear ratio of twelve to one.

The strike has a train of its own and is independently powered by its own weight. Nevertheless it is controlled by the time train in that once every hour a pin in the face of the center wheel raises a lever in the strike mechanism, and when the lever falls the strike train is released.

The speed at which a strike, chime or musical train is allowed to run must be governed, otherwise the weight will fall quickly causing the hammers to function rapidly. The necessary braking effect was accomplished by fitting a small fan, known as a fly, at the end of the train. In this position the fly is driven at high speed and the resultant air resistance is sufficient to produce the required steadying effect.

If the purchase of a grandfather clock is under consideration, it will be necessary to establish the quality of the clock together with its age and condition before a price can be determined. The responsibility for safe transportation would rest with the dealer if it were a dealer making the sale. If the purchase were of a private nature, the responsibility would be that of the buyer.

The contents of this chapter will assist in determining the quality and age of the clock, but to arrive at an assessment of condition a close inspection is desirable. General notes dealing with the inspection of clocks and the preparation for transportation will be found in Chapter Ten.

Dates of Interest

1659 Grandfather clocks first appeared.

1660 Eight-day and month duration movements established.

1661 Bolt-and-shutter introduced.

1669 Popularity of coffin clock ended. Side windows of hoods ceased to be necessarily the same height as front windows.

1671 William Clement first used the anchor escapement.

1675 Long pendulums appeared. Marquetry was introduced.

1676 Rack striking was invented by Dr. Edward Barlow and introduced by Thomas Tompion.

1680 Domed tops introduced and case heights reached seven feet. Cases were by now decorated with intricate designs.

1685 Hoods were made to slide forward. The Greek

pediment had almost disappeared.

1690 Eleven inch dials in use. Chiming clocks in regular use.

1695 Tompion devised mechanical means of indicating equation of time. Appearance of break-arch dial to accommodate the equation of time indicator mounted on top of the movement. First of such clocks produced by Tompion for William III.

1710 Rack striking moved from between plates and fitted between dial and front plate. Marquetry remained fashionable; the most popular designs were arabesque. Signatures appeared in the center of dials.

1720 Bolt-and-shutter rarely fitted after this time. Cases decorated with figured or burr walnut. Trunk doors with shaped tops appeared.

1725 The attention that had been given to movement plates and plate pillars began to wane. Half-hour ornaments and quarter-hour division rings almost disappeared.

1730 Moon dials appeared. All-over lacquer work appeared. Decline in popularity of grande sonnerie.

1740-1760 Very few grandfather clocks made.

1750 Center seconds hands and serpentine minute hands in use. Lift up hoods were discontinued.

1752 England adopted Gregorian calendar; equation work rarely fitted after this date.

1760 Provincial clockmakers carried on making grandfather clocks, while London clockmakers concentrated on bracket clocks. Solid mahogany was used without veneer or other decoration for low-priced clocks. Popularity of lacquer work had finished; very little produced after this time. Carving introduced as part of main structure of hood. Less attention given to hands. Brass break-arch dials with engraved and silvered centers appeared.

1770 Chiming and musical movements with four trains were made, necessitating larger hoods and cases.

1775 White painted iron dials fitted to cheap clocks.

1785 Brass dials with dots in minute ring appeared.

CHAPTER 6

English Bracket Clocks (1658-1850)

IT has been said in Chapter Five that after John Fromanteel returned to London from Holland in 1658 with the knowledge he had gained in Saloman Coster's workshop, the Fromanteel family immediately began making pendulum clocks. Their lead was closely followed by other London clockmakers.

That same year the first English made spring-driven pendulum clocks appeared in London and they became known as bracket clocks. They were not, as the name suggests, clocks to be placed necessarily on brackets like their predecessors the weight-driven lantern clocks. Instead, they were portable clocks and usually stood on tables or mantels. There are different explanations offered as to why they were so named, but whatever the reason, the name has been universally accepted.

Bracket clock movements were basically the same as those in grandfather clocks, except for the source of motive power. (See Chapter Five.) Their few differences are discussed in this chapter. Similarly, almost everything that has been said about grandfather clock dials and hands applies equally to bracket clocks.

A considerable amount of development took place during the last quarter of the seventeenth century, but bracket clocks remained popular for two hundred years, during which time there were other changes.

To assist in identifying the age of an English bracket clock it is necessary to follow the development in some detail; to this end their span of popularity has been divided into periods roughly proportionate to their rate of development, i.e. 1658-1670, 1671-1700, 1701-1750, and 1751-1850.

1658-1670

The design of the very earliest bracket clocks was that of restrained simplicity. They were rectangular in shape with lockable full width glazed doors at the front and the back, and a glass panel in each side. A triangular Greek pediment was mounted on the top. The cases were made of wood, usually oak veneered with ebony, but some were of olive wood or lignum-vitae stained black. They were completely without ornamentation which emphasized the austerity of their appearance.

Almost all movements had a duration of eight days between windings and they were fitted with fusees and verge escapements with short bob pendulums. A few timepieces were made but the majority were clocks with hour striking. In some instances the mechanism was arranged to provide a single strike at each half-hour, either on the hour bell or on an additional bell. Quarter-hour striking in this period was very rare.

Up to 1669 the time and strike winding holes in the dials were positioned close to the Roman numerals X and II but after that date the position of the holes became inconsistent.

The fitting of calendar work was not uncommon in the earliest bracket clocks and the practice continued well into the eighteenth century. Very few clocks of any period were fitted with seconds hands. Some early clocks were made with alarm discs and the method of setting was as described for lantern clocks in Chapter Four.

An examination of an original movement from this period will reveal that the plate pillars are riveted to the front plate. The reduced diameters of the opposite ends of the pillars pass through holes in the back plate, where they are held by taper pins.

(Left).
Figure 60. A very early 8-day ebony veneered bracket clock with pediment top. Gilt dial, silvered chapter ring, alarm and Dutch strike. Signed Edward East. Circa 1665.

(Right)
Figure 61. An early 8-day ebonized wood bracket clock with pediment top. Engraved gilt dial with silvered chapter ring. Dutch strike. Signed William Clement. Circa 1670.

(Center)
Figure 62. An early 8-day ebonized wood bracket clock with pediment top and Jacobean pillars. Gilt dial and silvered chapter ring. Calendar and strike. Signed Joseph Knibb. Circa 1670.

104

Unlike clocks made at a later period, the back plates of the earliest clocks were rarely decorated with engraving except for an elaborate signature of the clockmaker. Sometimes the strike locking plates were engraved with floral and leaf or Tudor rose, but otherwise the back of the movement was plain.

Night timepieces were made during this period. They consisted of a painted dial, usually depicting a religious scene, with a semi-circular or semi-eliptical slot cut in the upper half. Behind the dial was a set of hour circles that were caused to rotate in succession, each one having an hour numeral pierced and backed with silk. An oil lamp was placed inside the case and the light shone through the silk illuminating the numeral. The time taken for the numeral to travel from one end of the slot to the other was one hour; the number of minutes past the hour could be either estimated according to the position of the numeral along the slot, or the number of minute divisions could be read from the main dial. Some cases were fitted with a chimney to release heat and smoke.

It was not uncommon to fit gut pallets to the escapement and to cut symmetrical triangular teeth on the escape wheel to provide silent operation. The gut wore through but it was easy to renew.

1671-1700

During the early years of this period architectural style cases were made in a more decorative form but fewer in number, and cases with dome tops were introduced.

The width of pediment topped cases was increased to make room for a pillar at each side of the dial door. At first the pillars were spiraled after the fashion of Jacobean and then came plain Corinthian columns with gilt bases and acanthus capitals. The very best of the architectural clocks had four pillars or columns, one in each corner. In some instances the base was fitted with a central boss and spigot so that the clock could be turned without being lifted. Some of these cases had a gilt escutcheon in the tympanum of the pediment and the

Figure 63. 8-day ebonized wood bell top bracket clock with a very rare dial. Roman strike, evidence of which is the numeral IV. Each minute division is numbered. Tic-tac escapement. Alarm and calendar. The cord at the side is for winding the alarm. Signed Joseph Knibb, London. Circa 1675.

Figure 64. Back plate of a bracket clock by William Speakman, London. Circa 1680.

top was frequently surmounted by three gilt finials.

Oak veneered with ebony continued to be the most popular material and finish, and remained so for very many years after its use was discontinued in the making of English grandfather clock cases.

In the meantime changes were made to the design of the top. In place of the pediment some cases had panels of wood placed one above the other in terrace form and then finials were added, usually one in each corner and one in the center. This, however, was not a design that lasted long because it

107

soon gave way to the introduction of a dome top, variations of which continued into the nineteenth century.

Carrying handles and dome tops were introduced about the same time. One wonders if the original architectural clocks were intended to be used on wall brackets which would explain the absence of handles on the case, the lack of decoration on the movement back plate, and the reason for their name.

It is probable that owners of these clocks found it convenient to move them from room to room, as required, and casemakers would be expected to fit carrying handles. If this were so, then the Greek pediment had to go to make way for a design of top where the fitting of a handle was made possible.

Under these conditions the clock was fully portable and as such could quite easily stand in the center of a table and be seen from any angle. This would explain why back plates became so ornately engraved.

The first dome tops were rarely more than one and a half inches tall. They were known as bell tops, and when they were introduced the pillars or columns were omitted and the doors once again were made to span the full width of the case.

Unlike the earliest clock cases that were without any form of ornamentation, the new bell top bracket clocks were frequently embellished with carefully pierced and chased gilt metal frets on the dome. Escutcheon plates were fitted to keyholes and invariably matching escutcheons would be positioned opposite to balance the appearance. The top rail of the door was sometimes cut into a fret and backed with silk. This form of decoration was also applied to the panel above the side windows. Turned metal finials were frequently used, one at each corner of the top, and the use of turned metal feet was quite usual at this period. Without exception every clock had a pivoted metal handle secured to the dome. Clocks of high quality were often decorated with silver handles and ornaments.

By 1680 cases were being made with the bell top completely covered with pierced metal; these were known as basket tops. A few years later the double basket was introduced. This was a bell top rising from the clock case on a concave section and surmounted by a panel and a second bell top.

About 1685 casemakers began fitting metal frets to the side panels instead of using glass windows, and the top rails of doors were decorated with pierced metal ornaments.

Up to 1675 clockmakers had their names engraved along the bottom edge of the dial plate but the engraving was frequently obscured by the bottom rail of the door when closed. After this date signatures were raised to a more prominent position.

Towards the end of the seventeenth century a number of cases were veneered with mother-of-pearl or tortoise shell,

(Left)
Figure 65. 8-day ebonized wood bracket clock with gilt dial and silvered chapter ring. Calendar and Dutch strike. Signed Joseph Knibb, Londini Fecit. Circa 1680.

(Center)
Figure 66. 8-day ebony veneered bracket clock with gilt dial and silvered chapter ring. Bolt-and-shutter, calendar, pull quarter repeat, and strike. Signed Thomas Tompion. Circa 1680.

(Right)
Figure 67. 8-day ebonized striking bracket clock with basket top and ormolu mounts. Gilt dial, silvered zone and calendar. Signed Henricus Harpur, London. Circa 1682.

(Left)
Figure 68. 8-day ebony veneered striking bracket clock with bell top. Gilt dial, silvered chapter ring and calendar. Signed James Clowes. Circa 1685.

(Center)
Figure 69. 8-day ebonized wood bracket clock with basket top and ormolu mounts. Inside locking plate strike, with strike-silent control at top of dial above 60. Signed Joseph Knibb. Circa 1685.

(Right)
Figure 70. 8-day ebony veneered bracket clock with gilt dial and silvered chapter ring. Plain bell top. Calendar and strike with strike-silent control above 60 at top of dial. Signed Thomas Tompion. Circa 1685.

but these methods of decoration were never as popular as the ebonized finish.

About 1690 mock pendulums were fixed to the forward ends of verge staffs and the dial plates were cut with a curved slot so that the swinging bob of the false pendulum was visible. This arrangement provided an immediate visual indication as to whether or not the clock was going.

Early in this period many clockmakers reversed the method of securing the plate pillars. The new method was to rivet them to the back plate and pin them to the front plate. A refinement to the pinning method was to turn a groove at the end of the pillar and lock the assembly by means of a hinged latch.

(Upper Left)
Figure 71. 8-day ebony bracket clock with decorated bell top. Verge escapement, strike and strike-silent control at top of dial above 60, and pull quarter repeat mechanism. Height 12 inches. Signed Joseph Knibb, London. Circa 1695.

(Right)
Figure 72. 8-day ebony veneered bracket clock. Gilt dial and silvered chapter ring. Pull quarter timepiece. Signed Thomas Tompion. Circa 1686.

(Lower Left)
Figure 73. 8-day ebonized ship's cabin timepiece with swivel top. Gilt dial, silvered chapter ring and calendar. Signed George Allet, London. Circa 1696.

111

In 1675 makers began decorating movement back plates with engraving in varying degrees of complexity ranging from simple scrolls of foliage or the popular tulip pattern, to most ornate designs of leafy scrolls and flowers, often featuring cherubs at each side of the signature plaque. The final touch of extravagance was the fitting of beautifully executed pierced and chased metal cocks to cover the pendulum suspensions.

By this time the anchor escapement was being used in grandfather clocks in conjunction with long pendulums. This arrangement responded well to positive and accurate positioning of the clock, but any misalignment of the case or subsequent change of attitude would cause the movement to function out of beat which invariably resulted in stopping the clock.

This sensitivity did not apply to verge escapements and, because of their portability, bracket clocks continued to be fitted with verge escapements.

There was, however, an attempt by Tompion, a little after 1670, to obtain the advantages offered by an anchor escapement; this he did by designing what was called the tic-tac escapement. It was an anchor the length of which was reduced to span only two teeth of the escape wheel instead of the usual seven. It appears not to have been completely successful because it was rarely used after 1680.

Reference has been made in Chapter Five to the invention of rack striking in 1676 by Dr. Edward Barlow. This new method of striking was applied to grandfather clocks and bracket clocks, but shortly afterwards Dr. Barlow invented a repeater mechanism which was used only on bracket clocks.

These clocks were placed at the bedside. If the room were in darkness when the occupant wanted to know the time, instead of having to light a candle or oil lamp, all that was necessary was to pull a cord that hung from the side of the case. The cord was attached to the lifting piece of the strike mechanism and when it was pulled the lifting piece was raised which set the strike mechanism in motion. The previous hour followed by the previous quarter was then sounded. For convenience, two cords were supplied, one on

Figure 74. Left hand clock. 8-day ebony veneered bracket clock with pull quarter repeat. Height 12 inches. Signed Thomas Tompion, London. Clock No. 55. Circa 1687.
Right hand clock. 8-day ebony veneered striking bracket clock. Seconds and strike-silent subsidiary dials in upper spandrels. Pull quarter repeat and mock pendulum. Height 9 1/2 inches. Signed Thomas Tompion, London. Clock No. 270. Circa 1697.

each side of the case. On rare occasions only one cord was fitted and this was taken from beneath the case.

To prevent unnecessary striking during the night it was common practice to use timepieces instead of clocks; because there was no strike train to provide the energy to operate the repeat mechanism, a spring was introduced that was wound by the action of pulling the cord. Clocks with repeat mechanism were sometimes fitted with a locking plate for striking and a rack for the repeat.

With the introduction of the long pendulum to the grandfather clock, adjustment by means of screwing the bob up or

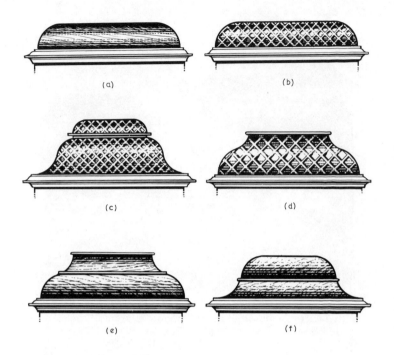

Figure 75. Bracket clock case tops.
(a) bell 1671
(b) basket 1680
(c) double basket 1685
(d) bell shaped basket 1701
(e) inverted bell 1705
(f) true bell 1730

down was not a difficult task, but this was not so with the bracket clock.

When a bracket clock was used on a mantel, or against a wall, it had to be lifted away and turned round to open the door at the back. The bob was usually swinging in the well of the case and not easy to reach.

About 1685 Tompion introduced an arrangement to overcome this problem. The suspension spring at the top of the

114

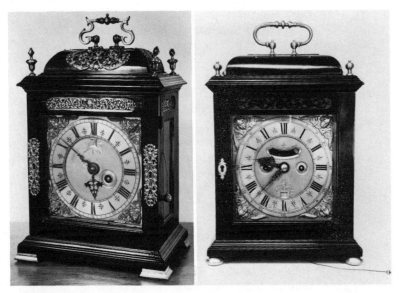

(Left)
Figure 76. 8-day ebonized bracket clock. Pull quarter timepiece. Calendar. Gilt dial and silvered chapter ring. Gilt finials and applied ornaments. Circa 1695.

(Right)
Figure 77. 8-day ebonized striking bracket clock with mock pendulum. Calendar and pull quarter repeat. Signed Peter Garon, London. Circa 1700.

pendulum rod was positioned between a pair of fixed brass blocks placed close together. Above the blocks was a movable carriage to which was secured the top of the spring. By raising or lowering the carriage the effective length of the pendulum below the fixed blocks was shortened or lengthened accordingly. This eliminated the difficulty experienced in trying to reach the bob.

To dispense with the need of having to turn the clock round to provide access through the door at the back, Tompion arranged for the position of the pendulum carriage to be adjusted from the front of the clock. This he did by fitting a regulator hand and subsidiary dial in one of the upper spandrels. When the hand was turned with its arbor, the carriage was made to move. This arrangement is known as rise and fall.

The appearance of the main dial was balanced by fitting a similar subsidiary dial in the opposite spandrel which carried a strike-silent hand. By selection of the hand the strike could be effectively silenced.

The diameter of these subsidiary dials required more space on the dial plate than had previously been occupied by spandrel ornaments and so it became necessary to increase the height of the main dial.

During this period bolt-and-shutter maintaining power was occasionally used.

Near the end of the seventeenth century clocks with musical and chiming movements were becoming popular. Dutch striking and grande sonnerie were introduced about the same time as for grandfather clocks.

During the latter part of the seventeenth century and the early years of the eighteenth century, the quality of craftsmanship and the balance of design reached their peak; for these reasons, in addition to their age, they are the most valued among bracket clocks.

1701-1750

At the turn of the century England was engaged in an export trade to Turkey and the merchandise included clocks. This trade increased steadily during the opening years and by about 1745 a considerable quantity of clocks was being made specially for this market. Among the most notable of the clockmakers were Markwick Markham and Christopher Gould.

The first of these clocks followed the conventional design of bracket clocks except that tortoise shell and lacquer were the most favored finishes. The cases were decorated with gilt or silver mounts and supported on cast scrolled feet. The top was usually the true bell pattern with a finial at each corner. Turkish numerals were engraved within the chapter ring.

(Upper Left)
Figure 78. 8-day ebonized bracket clock with basket top. Pull quarter timepiece. Turned brass finials. Circa. 1710.

(Right)
Figure 79. 8-day ebonized bracket clock with rich gilt mounts and escutcheons. Inverted bell top and frets to sides. Calendar dial in break-arch. Rise and fall, and strike-silent subsidiary dials in upper spandrels. Seconds in center zone of dial. Signed Daniel Quare, London. Circa 1715.

(Lower Left)
Figure 80. 8-day lacquered timepiece with mock pendulum. Signed John Ellicott, London. Circa 1720.

Figure 81. 8-day ebonized striking bracket clock with true bell top, ormolu mounts and turned brass finials. Silk backed frets at sides. Strike-silent subsidiary dial in break-arch. Gilt dial, silvered chapter ring, mock pendulum and calendar. Signed J. Pepys, London. Circa 1730.

Figure 82. A rare and fine specimen of an 8-day walnut three-train grande-sonnerie bracket clock. Gilt dial, silvered chapter ring, mock pendulum and calendar. Revolving turntable, ormolu mounts and inverted bell top. Strike-silent subsidiary dial in break-arch. Signed John Ellicott, London. Circa 1735.

Figure 83. 8-day ebonized bracket clock with inverted bell top and glass side panels. Pull quarter timepiece with verge escapement. Gilt dial with silvered chapter ring. Calendar in break-arch, and mock pendulum. Height to top of handle 17^1/$_2$ in. Engraved and signed back plate John Berry, London. Circa 1740.

During the second half of the eighteenth century these clocks became more grand and ornate, and some were topped with a cupola dome completely covered with pierced and chased metal. Many of these clocks were fitted with chime movements, and built-in musical boxes were particularly popular.

Returning to clocks made for the English market, there was very little change in design during the first half of the eighteenth century. It seems that about 1700 this style of clock had almost reached the end of its development period.

The ebonized finish continued to be the most popular, but casemakers showed a preference for the use of pearwood instead of oak for the ground work because of its ability to assume a high polish. A few lacquered cases were made and walnut cases were not uncommon.

The break-arch dial was introduced about 1710 and the additional dial space was usually occupied by a subsidiary dial for strike-silent or calendar.

Towards the end of this period dials were made without the half-hour and quarter-hour divisions.

1751-1850

The traditional style of bracket clock continued with little change well into the eighteenth century, but in the meanwhile, there appeared a new style in a variety of forms which were almost entirely without metal ornamentation.

The first indication came about 1750 when cases with inverted or true bell tops appeared with round dial windows in the full width doors instead of the usual break-arch windows. The cases were plain wood with a carrying handle on top. Ebonizing continued to be the most popular finish, but casemakers were beginning to use mahogany and walnut. Dials were silvered until, towards the end of the eighteenth century, plain white enameled round dials were being fitted.

The balloon clocks appeared about 1760. These had arch tops and incurved sides making the cases narrow waisted. Sometimes the cases were surmounted by a form of inverted bell top with a turned brass finial, and side handles were

(Upper Left)
Figure 84. 8-day ebony veneered strike and chime bracket clock. Mounted with ormolu on a gilt metal bracket, gilt dial and silvered chapter ring. Rise and fall, and strike-silent subsidiary dials in break-arch. Calendar aperture. Signed Eardley Norton, London. Circa 1760. There is a similar clock in Buckingham Palace by the same maker.

(Right)
Figure 85. 8-day ebonized striking bracket clock with true bell top. Strike-silent, and rise and fall subsidiary dials in break-arch. Gilt dial, silvered chapter ring and calendar. Signed Thomas Hill, Fleet Street, London. Circa 1765.

(Lower Left)
Figure 86. 8-day tortoise shell bracket clock with strike, chime, and musical mechanism. Cupola top and pierced ormolu plaques and mounts. Gilt dial, silvered chapter ring, and chime-not chime, and tune selection subsidiary dials in break-arch. Signed Markwick Markham. Circa 1775.

122

Figure 87. 8-day ebonized striking bracket clock. Inverted bell top, side handles, ormolu caryatids and mounts, and gilded feet and finials. Gilt dial with silvered chapter ring, calendar, and strike-silent dial in break-arch. Movement with verge escapement and engraved back plate. Height 25 inches to top of center finial. Signed Charles Penton, London. Circa 1775.

Figure 88. 8-day bracket clock made for the Turkish market. The striking and musical movement plays four tunes on eight bells. Circular white enameled dials, the surround decorated with medallions and formal stems on blue enamel ground enclosed in an arched case. Surmounted by a domed cupola veneered with tortoise shell and mounted with pierced ormolu plaques, foliage mounts to angles and supports, vase shaped finials and scroll feet. With travelling case. Signed Markwick Markham, Perigal, London. Circa 1775.

124

Figure 89. 8-day ebonized striking bracket clock. Gilt dial with silvered chapter ring, strike-silent in break-arch, and calendar. True bell top and glass side panels. Signed James Tregent, Leicester Square, London. Circa 1775.

125

(Upper Left)
Figure 90. 8-day ebonized striking bracket clock with pull quarter repeat on six bells. Gilt dial, silvered chapter ring, calendar, mock pendulum and strike-silent in break-arch. Verge escapement and engraved back plate. Height 16 inches. Signed Wm. Hughes, London. Circa 1780.

(Right)
Figure 91. George III mahogany 8-day striking bracket clock. Maker William Webster, London. Circa 1780.

(Lower Left)
Figure 92. 8-day mahogany striking bracket clock. Gilt dial, silvered chapter ring, calendar and strike-silent in break-arch. True bell top with fret side panels. Signed Samuel Cleghorn, London. Circa 1785.

126

(Upper Right)
Figure 93. George III mahogany 8-day striking bracket clock. Gilt dial, silvered chapter ring, calendar and strike-silent in break-arch. Fret side panels and break-arch top. Signed Fra. Robotham, Hampstead. (Francis Robotham, Hampstead, London). Circa 1790.

(Left)
Figure 94. Engraved back plate with Prince of Wales feathers. See Figure 93.

(Lower Right)
Figure 95. George III 8-day mahogany striking bracket clock with boxwood stringing. Verge escapement. White enamel dial with unusual calendar dial. Height 16 inches. Signed Jno. Ashley, London. (John Ashley) Circa 1790.

Figure 96. George III 8-day inlaid satinwood bracket clock with break-arch top and side handles. Quarter chiming. Musical with choice of seven tunes: God Save the King, Miss Baks, Hornpipe, Dusky Night, Mrs. Casey, La Belle Catherine, Captain Macintosh, and 107th Psalm. Signed De Lafons, Royal Exchange, London. Circa 1800.

Figure 97. Movement of clock in Figure 96. Note the fine finish and attention to detail.

129

(Upper)
Figure 98. A Regency style ebonized 8-day striking bracket clock. Small strike-silent lever at top of white enamel dial close to bezel. Signed James McCabe, Royal Exchange, London. Circa 1830.

(Lower)
Figure 99. Left hand clock. Regency mahogany bracket clock with brass inlay and painted dial. Pierced brass fret side panels and brass acorn finial. Double fusee movement with engraved back plate and pendulum. Height 20$\frac{1}{2}$ inches. Maker Robert Roskell, Liverpool. Circa 1815.

Right hand clock. Victorian rosewood bracket clock with double fusee movement. Height 17$\frac{1}{2}$ inches. Maker Frodsham, Grace-church St., London. Circa 1840.

130

frequently used. The dials were round and white enameled and secured direct to the case. A round domed glass, the same diameter as that of the dial, was held in a brass bezel or ring to which was attached a small brass hinge. The glass was thus allowed to swing away from the dial to permit winding of the springs and setting of the hands.

By 1770 the inverted bell and the true bell were replaced by a break-arch top, the shape of which followed the contour of the break-arch window in the full width door. The case was provided with a handle at the top. By 1800 the curve of the break-arch top had become more pronounced and the top handle had been replaced by side handles. Round white enameled dials were in use and the full width door had been discontinued in favor of a round glass in a hinged brass bezel.

During the first decade of the nineteenth century three more forms of the new style appeared. The first of these was a case with a chamfered panel top surmounted by a gilt finial and fitted with side handles; then came the lancet with its narrow pointed arch as in a lancet window, and lastly the arch top with straight sides. The latter was frequently ornamented with a form of inverted bell top with finial. All three types of clock had round white enameled dials secured to the cases and protected by circular domed glasses in round metal bezels.

At the end of the eighteenth century a few casemakers began to reintroduce the use of metal frets, particularly in side panels. Brass inlay work became popular, and Arabic numerals marking minute divisions began to disappear.

All these new forms of bracket clock continued to be made well into the nineteenth century each with its own variants.

CHAPTER 7

Black Forest Clocks (1650-1842)

THE Black Forest is in the south west corner of Germany in the provinces of Baden and Wurttemberg bordering on France and Switzerland. It is now an important industrial area engaged in the production of clocks.

Clockmaking started among farmworkers somewhere about 1650 and, at the time, there was a small industry producing glassware. During the winter months there was insufficient work to keep the farmworkers fully employed and they looked for other means of earning a wage.

A few enterprising clockmakers recognized the opportunity of making money and they employed farmworkers to make clock parts, often in their own homes, for very little money, and then sold the assembled clocks for a handsome profit.

The different parts were made by different families so that each group of people became skilled at making one component and nothing else. This speeded up the work and at the same time made it difficult for any one worker to produce clocks on his own and become a competitor.

Each master clockmaker had his own styles and standards and the parts used in his clocks would not necessarily be suitable for use in a movement made by another clockmaker.

The basic design was that of a lantern clock except that almost all the parts, including the frames and wheels, were made of wood, usually beech. Wheel pivots were made of short lengths of iron wire pushed into the ends of the wooden wheel arbors.

As with the lantern clock movement there were two horizontal plates mounted one above the other and separated by four corner posts. Vertical strips of wood, positioned one behind the other and supported between the upper and lower plates, were drilled to provide bearings for the wheel pivots. The wooden dials were painted, usually white with black Roman numerals and minute track, and outside the circle were colored floral designs.

The movement was driven by a weight hanging from a cord and controlled by a short bob pendulum and foliot and verge escapement.

There was no change of any consequence to the design of the movement until the eighteenth century when, about 1720, a striking train was added. The clockmakers took advantage of local resources and had the strike bells made of glass.

About this time arched dials were introduced. They were frequently covered with paper and then painted instead of the paint's being applied directly to the wood.

In 1730 the cuckoo clock was invented. The device consisted of a small bird carved from wood and painted, and two wind pipes operated by bellows, one to sound the 'cuc' and the other to sound the 'koo'. On the hour a small door opened above the dial; the cuckoo popped out and opened its beak each time the pipes sounded the hour. The mechanism consisted of a simple but ingenious system of bent wires and was adaptable to any of the Black Forest wall clocks being made at the time.

About 1750 the anchor escapement and the long pendulum began to appear, but even so clocks with the verge escapement were still being made in the early nineteenth century.

Brass founding began about 1780 and this enabled the clockmakers to have wheels cast and then turned. Very few clocks were afterwards made with wooden wheels. The casting of brass made it possible to use metal bells and so the practice of fitting glass bells was discontinued.

Figure 100. A 19th century Black Forest 12-hour cuckoo clock with painted shield dial and striking movement.

Towards the end of the eighteenth century chains began to replace the cords for hanging the time and striking weights but cords continued in use for alarm weights. In the early nineteenth century the time and strike trains were positioned side by side instead of one behind the other, and strike bells were replaced by coiled wire gongs.

Although the clocks were individually made, large quantities were produced and the clockmakers employed traveling salesmen who toured Europe selling and taking orders. Business grew and by the early nineteenth century a thriving export market had been created. This situation continued until 1842 when Chauncey Jerome began to export factory-made clocks from America at prices lower than had hitherto been possible. This had the effect of bringing clock production in the Black Forest to a standstill.

The clockmakers were quick to realize that if their industry were to survive they had to follow the American lead and turn their attention to mass production. This they did and by 1850 the industry had recovered from its temporary setback. Many of the American clocks were copied and it is not always easy to identify one from the other.

In 1870 a new style of cuckoo clock was produced and it immediately became very popular. The design has remained almost unchanged for over a century. It is the cuckoo clock that we know today and is a great favorite among tourists to the Black Forest.

Other very popular novelties with visitors are the reproductions of early Black Forest clocks complete with foliot and verge escapements.

CHAPTER 8

American Clocks (1680-1845)

AMONG the early settlers from England, France, Spain, Holland and Sweden were blacksmiths and locksmiths many of whom had a knowledge of clockmaking, but unfortunately we know nothing about these men. The oldest known records date back no further than the late seventeenth century and even these contain only a handful of names.

Lists of clock and watch makers with dates have been compiled, but only after extensive research in public libraries, historical societies, state instutions, old church records and town directories, newspapers and periodicals, and from information supplied by private individuals. It was not until about 1800 that clock papers were printed with the maker's name and town glued inside the cases.

By 1680, when England led the world in horology, the majority of settlers in North America had come from England and clockmaking was beginning to get under way. Tools and raw materials were not plentiful and a great deal of improvisation was necessary. With the help of imports from England, these difficulties were slowly overcome.

Grandfather Clocks

Almost all clocks made during the years prior to the Revolution were grandfather clocks with eight-day brass movements produced by English craftsmen. The shortage of tools and materials so handicapped them that it was extremely difficult to maintain the standard of work that was associated with London.

The cases were simple and plain but even so they reflected English styling. The earliest were made of pine and walnut. They had paneled or plain rectangular doors; the hoods were flat topped and many had plain or twisted pillars flanking the dial opening. Dials were square and made of brass. Their design and subsequent development was much the same as in London, and clockmakers continued the practice of embellishing them with their signatures.

By 1700 hoods with bell tops were introduced. The year 1710 saw the appearance of the round top hood and about the same time trunk doors were made with shaped tops. The break-arch dial was introduced about 1720 and with it came the break-arch hood. More use was made of ornamentation. Turned wood and brass finials surmounted the top, and carving appeared on the trunks. That same year saw the start of an import business bringing cast brass movement parts from England; until then the clockmakers had been casting their own parts in small home-built foundries.

Chiming movements began to appear in 1740, and moon phase dials were introduced about 1745. In 1750 mahogany cases became popular and the scroll top was introduced. Carving on trunks remained popular and was extended to the fronts of hoods above the dials.

Cases decorated with marquetry or Japanning are rare.

During the years 1680-1770 the English styles prevailed. Then came the Revolution and clock production was almost non-existent and remained so until after the war. Little or no progress was made until about 1780 and then the presence of European and Scandinavian clocks began to have an influence on American-made clocks. New styles appeared and new ideas were exercised, but, even so, the quantity of grandfather clocks made during the sixty year period, 1780-1840, was far in excess of those made during the ninety years before the war.

Cases were made of cherry, curly maple, mahogany, pearwood, pine, walnut, and poplar which was usually painted or veneered. The trunks remained plain and without ornamentation but the quality of cabinetmaking was excellent. The majority of hood tops followed the English style of breakarch; more often than not they were surmounted by carved scroll work in the form of curly horns, or by 1790 a wood fret known as whales' tails. This particular hood pattern remained almost universal until about 1800. It was usual to complete the hood decoration by the addition of three finials which were either turned or cast brass, or carved or turned wood. The center finial brought the overall height of the case in some instances to nearly eight feet.

Turned or fluted columns or pillars flanked the dial opening and not infrequently they were fitted at the rear corners of the hood. These free standing pillars remained fashionable until about 1820.

The traditional English brass dial plate with its applied silvered and engraved chapter ring and spandrel ornaments disappeared during the war years. Its place was taken by a flat brass plate on which the numerals, spandrel ornaments and maker's name were engraved. Such dials were fitted to grandfather clocks up to about 1800.

The importing of cast brass parts from England was discontinued during the Revolution but by 1780 the trade had started again, and this time included some eight-day brass strike movements.

Seconds hands began to appear on some clocks, and the very best were fitted with sweep seconds hands. Visual indication that the clock was working was a popular idea and many dials were made with animated shapes in the breakarch for this purpose; the swinging of the pendulum was used to keep them in motion. Some of the more usual ones were a pitching boat, a blacksmith striking his anvil, an angler casting a line, children on a see-saw and a woodman sawing a log.

Some clockmakers experimented with short cases that measured between three feet and five feet in height. Only a few were made and they are now rare collectors' pieces. They were made to the same style as grandfather clocks but to a smaller scale; thus they retained the same pleasing proportions. They became known as grandmother clocks.

Instances have been known of grandfather clocks having had their cases cut and reduced to grandmother clock height. These acts of vandalism are immediately apparent from the squat ill-proportioned appearance of the cases.

The cost of making a grandfather clock case and fitting an eight-day brass strike movement was high and only a few families in each community were able to afford such a luxury. Nevertheless, every household needed to know the time and there was, therefore, a big demand for a low-priced clock.

This situation brought about the introduction of thirty-hour wooden strike movements. The wheels and frame plates were made of oak but the escape wheel continued to be made of brass and pivots and pinions of steel. The movements were supplied with dials, hands and weights and were known as hang-up clocks or wag-on-the-wall clocks.

This method of producing clocks resulted in a big reduction in cost, and to further the economy clockmakers supplied the movements without cases for use on shelves; the tall cases were purchased later, if required.

Brass dials began to disappear about 1790 in favor of imported white enameled dials from England and France. By 1800 there were almost no brass dials being made. Dials for low-priced clocks were made of painted metal and painted wood. Decoration in the spandrels took the form of animals, birds, fish, flowers and geometric patterns painted in a variety of colors. About 1792 paper dials were introduced for gluing direct to iron or wood dial plates for use on the cheapest clocks.

The days were fast disappearing when the cabinetmaker made the case and the clockmaker the movement. The making of dials and hands became specialized and men set themselves up as dialmakers and handmakers. Other men became wheel cutters, plate makers, turners and screwcutters, while the master clockmaker concentrated on assembling the parts. Such a situation must inevitably lead to some form of mass production.

One of the most famous names in the history of American horology is Eli Terry who, in the late eighteenth century, had started his career as a clockmaker producing grandfather clocks with eight-day brass movements. He was quick to realize that there was a very large market for low-priced movements which could never be satisfied by the slow rate of production from a system that produced one handmade movement at a time.

In 1800 Eli Terry started a factory at Plymouth, Connecticut. He equipped it with machinery and then diverted a nearby river to flow past his premises where he harnessed the energy to drive his machines. The venture had a limited success but he proved to himself that it was possible to increase considerably the rate of production of thirty-hour wooden movements at a cost much lower than had previously been possible.

Terry believed that with greater productive capacity he could further reduce the cost and so, in 1806, he sold his factory and bought an old water-mill. In 1807 he undertook a contract to manufacture four thousand wooden thirty-hour grandfather movements in three years. He recruited Seth Thomas and Silas Hoadley to assist him in what other clockmakers believed to be an impossible task. By 1810 the contract was successfully completed.

The pattern of grandfather clocks had become established and they continued to be made with little further change until about 1840, after which they made way for the new styles of clocks that we regard today as traditionally those of the United States of America.

Banjo Clocks

The name Willard is among the most prominent of early American clockmakers, and Simon was the most outstanding of three clockmaker brothers. In 1802 he took out a patent on a clock of his own design, the shape of which bore a strong resemblance to that of a banjo, from which it derived its name. The clock was an immediate success but, despite the

Figure 101. 8-day banjo wall timepiece with brass movement. Maker Aaron Willard. Circa 1810.

Figure 102. 8-day federal mahogany and parcel-gilded banjo bracket timepiece with brass movement. Height 33¹/₂ inches. Circa 1815.

existence of the patent, it was not long before other clock-makers were copying his idea; it would seem he took inadequate steps to safeguard his interests.

The clocks were originally designed to hang on a wall but such was their popularity that many were made to stand on a mantel or shelf.

The majority were without a strike train and should be referred to as timepieces, but in later years many were made with a strike mechanism in which case they are clocks. This complexity of naming is overcome if we refer to them all as clocks. Immediate identification is possible by the number of winding holes in the dial; a timepiece will have one whereas a clock will have two or more.

The case was generally made of mahogany. It had a round top into which was fitted a circular white enameled dial of slightly less diameter and which was painted with black Roman numerals and minute ring. The winding hole for the time train was situated close to the two o'clock position. In front of the dial was a convex glass held in place by a hinged narrow brass bezel or ring.

Mounted on the top was a single finial made of cast brass in a variety of shapes. Very popular until about 1815 was a brass eagle with outspread wings standing on a ball.

Beneath the round top was a slender trunk or neck that tapered outward and downward to a rectangular base with a hinged door. The front of the case was decorated with two painted glass panels, one on the trunk and the other on the base, and each was surrounded by a plain wood frame or wood moulding. The trunk panel was decorated with emblems, flowers, foliage and geometric patterns in gold and colors, usually against a white background, while the base panel displayed a scenic view or a design symbolic of seafaring days.

The ornamentation was completed by mounting against each side of the trunk a curved brass fret that extended from the underside of the round top to the upper surface of the rectangular base.

There were two variants of the banjo clock, the lyre and the girandole. The trunk of the lyre was shaped in the fashion of the musical instrument of that name and was usually framed in carved foliage or scroll work. Its head was the same as that of a banjo clock and from beneath the head a set of ornamental strings was frequently fitted which extended downward to the base of the trunk to complete the illusion of a string instrument.

Like the banjo clocks some were made to hang on a wall while others were intended to stand. Additional ornamentation was sometimes given to hanging clocks in the form of a carved bracket under the base of the trunk, and clocks intended for standing were provided with a flat base. In both types the front panel was delicately painted with floral patterns in gay colors.

The girandole was similar to the banjo except that the base was circular and carried small ornaments around its edge, reminiscent of a jewel studded pendant.

The movements in all these clocks were brass eight-day and driven by weights but, unlike the weights in a grandfather clock, those in a banjo had a short fall. To overcome the problem of limited endurance and give the movement a running time of eight days between winds, the line was wound onto a barrel of small diameter that carried a large main wheel. The gear ratio was such that the train was able to function with very little movement of the main wheel while allowing the weight to fall very slowly.

The position of the pendulum and crutch was an unusual feature of these movements for they were mounted immediately behind the dial. This was done to reduce the depth of the case to a minimum.

These clocks were artistically shaped and of pleasing proportions, and the decoration was in good taste. Their popularity lasted a little over half a century.

About 1840 the railroad companies began to use them in the stations, and some of the clock cases reached a height of seven feet.

Among dealers and collectors of old American clocks the banjo clocks rank second only to grandfather clocks, and the

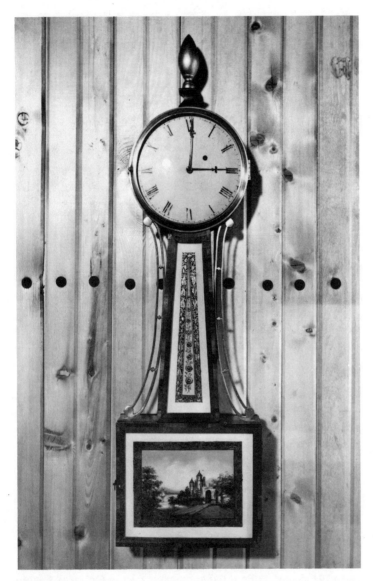

Figure 103. 8-day banjo wall timepiece with brass movement. Maker Simon Willard. Circa 1820.

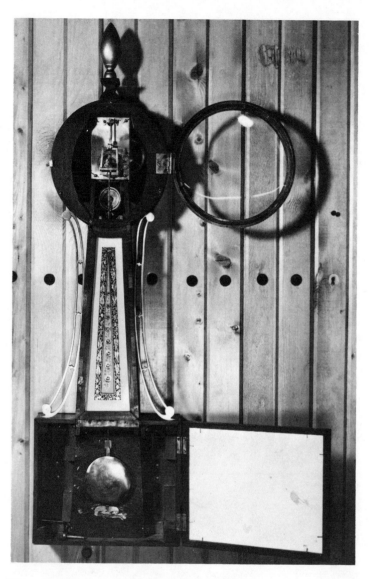

Figure 104. Simon Willard banjo clock, shown in Figure 103, with dial removed to show movement, and door opened to show pendulum bob.

most sought after are those which carry in the lower panel an inscription S. Willard. Patent.

Pillar And Scroll Clocks

Shortly after Eli Terry had successfully completed his contract to manufacture four thousand wooden thirty-hour weight-driven movements, he sold his water-mill clock factory to his two assistants, Seth Thomas and Silas Hoadley, and retired to a small workshop to experiment with his next idea.

As a result of his earlier success he was fast becoming a rich man. He had learned that simplicity of design, followed by a well planned mass-production method, was the only way to produce low-priced articles. Despite the large number of cheap wooden clock movements that had been made, and were still being made by other clockmakers, there remained an incalculable market for cheap clocks. Terry's next idea was to produce large quantities of cased wooden mantel clocks for as little as fifteen dollars and so, with this in mind, his experiments commenced.

During the next few years he produced many prototypes of which a few still exist and are known among collectors as Terry experimental clocks. By 1814 he produced a wooden-cased mantel clock that was readily adaptable to mass-production methods and which possessed all the characteristics he felt were necessary. In 1816 he took out a patent.

The clocks were an immediate success and they attracted other Connecticut clockmakers who were quick to seize the opportunity of taking part in what was obviously a profitable venture. Any building with a large ground floor area and nearby running water became desirable property overnight and offers were made and accepted for warehouses, public halls and chapels.

Eli Terry made his own cases as well as movements but he also sold movements to other clockmakers who fitted them into their cases under license. Thousands of clocks were produced and there were many variants of the standard Terry pillar and scroll clock.

Figure 105. 8-day pillar and scroll clock with wood movement by Seth Thomas. Circa 1822.

148

Figure 106. Seth Thomas pillar and scroll clock, shown in Figure 105, with door open to reveal movement and clock paper.

The cases were rectangular in shape and varied a little in size. The early ones were about twenty-eight inches high, fifteen inches wide and four inches deep and were made of solid or veneered mahogany. The doors covered the full width and height of the cases and they consisted of two panels, one above the other, enclosed within a narrow frame. The upper panel was square and glazed and behind it was mounted the square dial plate.

The lower panel of the door was a glass tablet on which was painted either a scenic view or a simple pattern. There was always an oval-shaped unpainted area in the center through which the bob of the pendulum could be observed.

Above the door was a scroll top in the form of a swan-neck pediment with three turned brass finials. Below the door the base was edged with a curved skirt which terminated in a small delicately shaped leg at each corner.

Either side of the door was a long, slender free-standing tapered pillar, the largest diameter being at the bottom.

The square dials were painted iron plates. The numerals were either Arabic or Roman, the former being the most usual, and colored designs were painted in the spandrels. Winding holes could be anywhere in the dial, and not necessarily symmetrical. The hands were delicately shaped and simple in design with very little pierced work.

Fig. 106 shows a Terry thirty-hour weight-driven wooden movement in a case by Seth Thomas. The back plate is a piece of oak spanning the full width of the case and forming part of the case back. The front plate is an assembly of mahogany strips located by four horizontal pillars extending from the back plate and held in place by taper pins. Wheels of these movements were made of walnut, cherry and mahogany, and apple wood was frequently used for pinions because of its hardness. Arbors or spindles were made of wood with a steel pivot driven into each end.

An entirely original idea of Eli Terry was to transfer the dial motion work from behind the dial to a position between the movement plates. The strike locking plate, the escapement and the pendulum were then brought from the

150

rear of the movement and positioned immediately in front of the movement front plate. This arrangement enabled the movement to be positioned well back inside the case.

In this movement the escapement anchor is positioned vertically against the right hand side of the escape wheel and is supported by a brass bracket mounted on the wooden frame. This bracket also provides the anchorage from which the pendulum is suspended and is the cause of the pendulum being off center. Such escapement arrangements are readily identifiable by the off center position of the clear glass window in the door tablet. The engagement between anchor and escape wheel can be adjusted by altering the position of the brass bracket.

The arrangement of lines and pulleys allows the weights to have maximum fall with an increased length of line resulting in the ability of a thirty-hour movement to function continuously for eight days without being rewound.

The strike mechanism is controlled by a locking plate which is positioned in front of the frame type front plate of the movement.

The label pasted inside the clock reads as follows:-

PATENT CLOCKS
Made and sold by
SETH THOMAS;
DIRECTIONS

For setting up and regulating said Clocks. Let the clock be set in a perpendicular position; this is necessary, in order to its having an equal beat; and if it fails to beat equally, it may be put in beat by bending the wire which receives the pendulum. If the clock goes too fast, lengthen the pendulum; but if too slow, shorten it by means of a screw at the bottom. If the hands want moving do it by means of the longest; turning at any time forward, but never backward; and if the clock fails to strike the proper hour, pull downward the small wire which hangs down under the face on the left side of the clock, and it will strike as often as you repeat the motion. Apply no oil at any time to it, unless it be a very small quantity of the oil of almonds, or sweet oil to the points of the teeth on the brass or crown wheel.

To wind up the weights, put the key on with the handle down, and turn it towards the figure 6. N.B. The public may be assured, that clocks made at the above factory, are equal, if not superior, to any made in the country.

Plymouth, Connecticut.

The standard Terry pillar and scroll cases were well proportioned, simple in design, and tastefully decorated, but it was not long before other casemakers departed from the original Terry design and produced cases of increased height with carved pillars and case tops.

About 1825 the bronzed looking-glass clock with brass movement was introduced by Chauncey Jerome, although records show that the patent was granted to Joseph Ives. The case was about six inches taller than the Terry clock and was decorated on top with carvings. The door was flanked on either side by a pair of carved half pillars, and a mirror was fitted in the lower panel in place of the painted glass tablet. The case was painted, and touched with gilt bronzing.

The clock was cheaper to produce but was sold for more than the Terry pillar and scroll. Many thousands were made and Jerome became a rich man. Around 1831, he began thinking of a design for a new type of clock.

So far, no American clockmaker had attempted to export clocks. It was thought impossible with wooden movements because the long sea voyage would cause the wood to swell and the clocks would be ruined. Jerome reasoned that a small inexpensive clock with a brass movement would find a ready market in America and abroad and so he turned his factory over to the production of thirty-hour brass clocks in wooden OG cases. The idea was a success and his business grew until,

Figure 107. 8-day federal mahogany pillar and scroll clock from Connecticut. Height 27¹/₂ inches. Circa 1830.

Figure 108. 8-day giant pillar and scroll mirror clock with brass movement in a cherry and maple case.

Figure 109. Movement of pillar and scroll clock shown in Figure 108.

155

in 1842, he shipped a consignment to England. The price was so low that the English import authorities thought the goods were being dumped and they seized the shipment and paid the invoice. When a second shipment arrived the same thing happened, but the arrival of the third consignment convinced the authorities that Jerome knew exactly what he was doing and the consignment was admitted. They were sold at prices much below any British clock. Shortly afterwards Jerome was shipping clocks to Europe and drove the Black Forest wall clocks off the market. The American export trade of clocks had become established.

Early in the nineteenth century it was apparent to clockmakers that the continued use of weights to drive their clocks was undesirable and that many advantages were associated with the use of coil springs as motive power. Good quality springs were very expensive and not easy to obtain; they had to be imported from Geneva or London. Even then, it was necessary that they be used with a compensating fusee.

About 1825 Joseph Ives invented an ingenious method of overcoming the problem of obtaining coil springs and at the same time dispensing with the need of a fusee. He introduced what became known as the wagon-spring movement which consisted of a leaf spring, bolted to the bottom of the clock case, that exerted a variable pull on chains which in turn pulled on lines wound round the wheel train barrels.

In Fig. 111 the device is shown in the wound position. Each end of the leaf spring is pulling downward on a yoke which engages a lever in one of a number of notches. The outer end of the lever swings about a pivot while the inner end is pulled downward bringing with it a chain. The upper end of the chain is secured to a drum which is fixed to a pulley spindle, and when the chain is unwound the drum and pulley rotate together.

Attached to the pulley is the lower end of a line. The upper end is secured to the barrel of the wheel train and when the pulley rotates, the line is pulled and the barrel turns.

By the selection of an alternative notch, the position of the yoke on the lever can be adjusted to provide an increase or

Figure 110. 8-day federal mahogany pillar and scroll clock from Connecticut. Height 30 inches. Circa 1830.

157

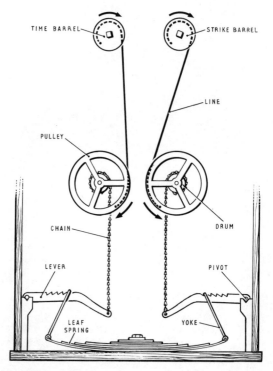

Figure 111. Motive power of a wagon-spring clock movement.

decrease in the amount of pull exerted by the leaf spring.

The ingenuity of the device lay in the arrangement of the lever and chain assembly which was designed to maintain a constant torque on the wheel train and escapement and thereby ensured that the pendulum swung with a regular beat.

After 1825 very little progress was made towards spring-wound clocks until 1843 when Charles Kirk introduced eight-day and thirty-hour movements driven by brass springs and fitted with cast-iron back plates. The unreliability of brass springs made it necessary to fit some form of guard to protect the movement from damage in the event of spring breakage and so the back plate was recessed to accommodate the springs. These spring-driven movements were first fitted

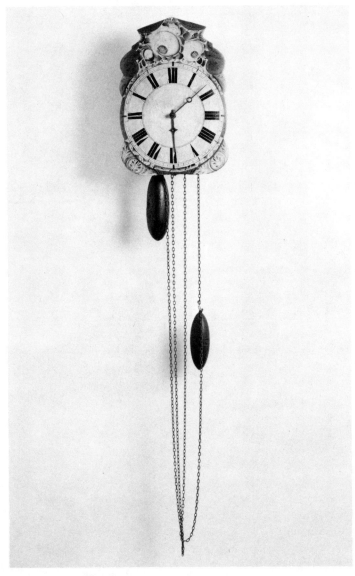

Figure 112. Painted wag-on-the-wall-clock. Diameter 13 1/2 inches. Circa 1820.

Figure 113. Left hand clock. 8-day lyre timepiece with brass movement. Maker J.C. Brown, Bristol, Connecticut. Circa 1850. Right hand clock. 8-day acorn clock with brass movement. Maker Forestville Manufacturing Co., Bristol, Connecticut.

Figure 114. Brass movement and fusees of acorn clock in Figure 113.

to round Gothic or beehive cases and sharp Gothic or steeple cases.

By 1845 steel springs were being produced. They were used with reverse fusees to drive eight-day brass movements. These movements were basically the same as those previously driven by weights and so the only change in the general arrangement was to substitute weight energy for spring energy.

The coiled springs were anchored to an arbor and housed in recesses cut in a wooden block that was located in the bottom of the case and secured to the back.

The reverse fusees were carried on the spring arbors and lines from the fusees were led upward and wound round the winding barrels of the movement.

The acorn clock, so named because of its shape, was one of the earliest to be driven in this way.

From 1845 onwards there was a rapid change from weight-driven to spring-driven clocks and after having served the colonists and the Americans for two hundred years the weight-driven clocks began to fade into obscurity.

Dates of Interest
Grandfather Clocks

1680-1770 Manufacture of English style clocks.
  Movements made of locally cast brass parts.
1700 Bell tops to hoods introduced.
1710 Round tops to hoods introduced.
  Trunk doors with shaped doors in use.
1720 Break-arch dials introduced.
  Break-arch hoods introduced.
  Carving appeared on trunks.
  Cast brass movements and parts imported from England.
1740 Chiming movements appeared.
1745 Moon phase dials appeared.
1750 Mahogany used for cases.
  Scroll tops introduced.
  Carving on fronts of hoods appeared.

1770-1840 Majority of clocks were made during this period. European and Dutch influences were apparent but fashionable English furniture styles retained some influence.

1774 Revolution.

1778 Original style of dial no longer made. New type of dial brought into use. Flat brass plate without applied spandrel ornaments. Numerals engraved, no applied chapter ring. All ornamentation and name of maker engraved directly onto flat brass plate. In use up to end of eighteenth century.

1783 Sweep seconds hands were in use.
Automata in the upper part of dial were becoming popular.

1790 Appearance of whales' tails on top of hoods.
Introduction of white enameled dials with painted decoration, and painted wooden dials. Both types of dials may or may not be painted with name of maker.

1792 Paper dials glued on iron or wood were introduced.

1800 Eli Terry introduced mass production of weight-driven wooden movements.

General

1780 New styles of clocks, other than grandfather clocks, began to appear.

1800 Clock papers introduced and glued inside cases.

1802 Simon Willard introduced banjo clocks.

1814 Eli Terry introduced pillar and scroll clocks.

1825 Joseph Ives introduced wagon-spring movements.
Chauncey Jerome introduced bronzed looking-glass clocks.

1842 Chauncey Jerome was first to export clocks.

1843 Charles Kirk introduced movements driven by brass springs.

1845 Steel springs were in use.
Acorn clock appeared.

CHAPTER 9

French Clocks (1643-1830)

THE manufacture of clocks in France during the Renaissance period reached a very high standard, so much so that France became one of the leading horological centers in Europe.

Many prominent French clockmakers were given positions in the royal courts and were appointed as clockmakers to the King.

During this period the French were very fashion conscious in regard to their furniture and it was customary among clockmakers to design their cases in the same style. It is of interest to note that the changes in furniture design closely coincide with the reigning periods of the kings of France; because of this it has become the accepted practice to describe the style by referring to the name of the monarch in whose reign the furniture was made. The same method of description is used in relation to French antique clocks.

The periods covered by this chapter are listed below.

Louis XIV	1643-1715	
Regency	1715-1723	
Louis XV	1723-1774	
Louis XVI	1774-1790	
Directoire	1795-1799	
Empire	1799-1804	Consulat
	1804-1815	Napoleon I
	1815-1824	Louis XVIII
	1824-1830	Charles X

164

Louis XIV

The first spring-driven pendulum clocks in France were mantel clocks which appeared about 1660 and were known as Religieuse. Despite the fact that Louis XIII had been dead some seventeen years when these clocks were first made they are nevertheless described as Louis XIII style, possibly because the clock cases were invariably ebonized, a finish that was popular with the court of his time.

The general design of the case was not unlike the early English architectural bracket clock. It was made of oak and veneered with ebony. At each side of the glazed door was a fluted pilaster with an acanthus capital. Sometimes these pilasters were made as part of the door. The arch on top of the case was fixed at the front and surmounted by three cast or turned metal finials, one in the center and one on either side. The cases were decorated with Boulle and corners were protected by gilt or ormolu mounts.

The rectangular iron dial plates were covered with velvet or silk and they filled the aperture behind the glass and obscured from view any part of the interior. The chapter rings were gilded or made of silver or pewter and secured on top of the dial plate cloth. It was not uncommon to find each minute division marked with a numeral. The hands were gilt and elaborately pierced. Immediately below the chapter ring and extending downward to the bottom edge of the door glass was a gilt ornament of scrolls and foliage or hanging tapestry.

Unlike a weight-driven clock when the energy of the falling weight remains constant, a spring-driven clock tends to lose some of its energy as the spring nears the point of being in need of rewinding. The fusee was invented to overcome this problem but such was the confidence that French clockmakers had in pendulum control that the fusee was rarely used. This was a contributory factor in the ability of the clockmakers to keep the size of their movements to a minimum.

Striking was by the locking plate method and remained so right through the nineteenth century.

The anchor escapement was never popular in France and

the verge escapement continued to survive long after other countries had discontinued its use.

There followed a period during which the Religieuse underwent some changes before it finally established itself about 1695 into the style that is traditionally known as Louis XIV.

The dial plate no longer reached to the bottom of the front aperture and it became possible for the first time to see the pendulum swinging behind the ornament under the chapter ring.

The distinctive architectural top disappeared and was replaced by a flat-topped dome with small figures at the front corners and two or three cast or turned finials on the platform. Close to the end of the century basket tops appeared supporting a figure, frequently one with wings and in a sitting posture, while at each corner of the platform was a small finial.

Whereas the glass aperture in the doors had been rectangular, they were subsequently given a new shape with semi-circular tops. Side windows that matched the new design were fitted making it possible to view the movement.

The simple gilt ornament of symmetrical pattern below the chapter ring was replaced by a larger ornament, frequently comprising one or more reclining figures.

The method of decorating the case remained much the same but the designs were more elaborate and practically every surface was covered, including the columns.

By the turn of the century the case tops were rounded. The line of the arch continued downwards to form waisted sides which curved outward at the base to support a sitting gilt figure at either side. Above the arch was a small central platform on which was mounted a third gilt figure.

The cases were made of oak and almost completely covered with Boulle decoration and ormolu ornamentation. Thin veneers of horn were sometimes used with colored designs and floral patterns painted on the back face. The horn was then mounted in ormolu surrounds. The glass front was set within a metal frame that followed the contours of the case,

Figure 115. Louis XIV bracket clock. Brass mounted case decorated with Boulle marquetry. Blue numerals on white enamel plaques. 8-day striking movement with outside locking plate. Height 36 inches. Maker Jacques Varin, Paris.

Figure 116. Louse XIV mantel clock decorated with Boulle marquetry. Dial with blue numerals on white plaques. 8-day striking movement. Maker F. Bualtoir.

Figure 117. Louis XIV mantel clock decorated with ormolu and red Boulle marquetry. 8-day striking movement. Dial with black numerals on white enamel plaques. Height 26 inches.

and through the glass the bob of the pendulum could be seen beneath the dial.

The circular dials became much smaller. The hour numerals were contained within separate enamel plaques on a background of gilt, and most, if not all, of the pierced decorative work disappeared from the minute hands. This type of clock became known as the Louis XIV Grand Style.

A development of the Religieuse appeared near the end of the reign of Louis XIV and lasted throughout the Regency period. It was a mantel clock a little taller than the Religieuse which stood about six feet from the floor on its own pedestal and plinth. The basic design of the clock case was much the same as the Religieuse and the movement retained the verge escapement and the short bob pendulum. The clock and the pedestal were made of oak and veneered with ebony and both were heavily and extravagantly decorated with Boulle and ormolu. These clocks were made only in France and at the end of the Regency period their popularity finished.

Regency

No new styles emerged during these eight years. The round-topped mantel clock cases with their waisted sides remained fashionable but the ormolu ornamentation of the bold baroque style developed into the more frivolous style of rococo.

The twelve enamel hour plaques of the Grand Style clock dials remained but an enamel center plate was introduced. They were known as thirteen-piece dials.

Louis XV

During the first ten years the Regency style was further developed, after which it assumed a more graceful and pleasing appearance. Narrowing of the case about its middle became more pronounced, and the base was made wider. The singular figure that invariably surmounted the earlier clocks was to a great extent replaced by a group of statuettes, while

Figure 118. Regency bracket clock decorated with Boulle marquetry and ormolu mounts. 8-day striking movement with 13 piece dial. Height 61 inches. Maker Lenoir, Paris.

171

the side figures disappeared and the ormolu work continued down to the plinth. The decoration remained in the rococo style but was less lavish than on Regency clocks.

While cases became more elaborate, the already small round movements and dials were made even smaller. Many dials had winding holes symmetrically placed.

The reduced wheels were cut with fine teeth, and the springs were fitted into going barrels. Heavy pendulums were frequently used to give greater control and improved timekeeping. The brass or gilded bobs were shaped to represent rays of the sun, a design which is known as sunburst. Many clocks had chime trains in addition to strike, and frequently a musical box was housed in the base of the clock case.

In 1730, Robert Martin and his brother introduced a finish that became known as Vernis Martin. It was an imitation Japanese lacquer that could be applied to rococo work as well as wood and it enabled rococo to be presented in a variety of colors. Its application to wood was usually carried out on a veneer of pearwood because its close grain provided a good foundation for the base color. In 1733 the two brothers were appointed wood polishers to the King.

Unlike England and most European countries, casemakers of France were given a status at least equal to that of clockmakers, and by 1750 it was a requirement of the casemakers' guild that all wood cases be inscribed with the name of the casemaker.

About 1755 French dialmakers found a way of making complete enamel dials and so it was not long before thirteenpiece dials completely disappeared.

By 1760 there was a definite trend towards the use of metal cases and castings of scroll work and foliage decorated with ormolu became popular. This was followed by the introduction of porcelain. The cast metal base supported a group of porcelain figures above which was mounted the dial.

A delicate and artistically arranged porcelain floral display surrounded the figures and the dial. These clocks are much sought after by collectors and if in a good condition will

Figure 119. Louis XV mantel clock. 8-day striking movement and 13 piece dial in a brass case mounted on a bronze elephant and brass base. Height 17¹/₂ inches.

173

usually fetch a high price on the open market.

During the reign of Louis XV a wall clock appeared in France called the cartel. Some were cast in brass, or in a base metal decorated with ormolu, while others were made of carved wood.

The frames consisted of scrolls and foliage, typical of rococo, and surmounted by a figure or group of figures, or had architectural characteristics with pineapple and flambeau finials and festooned with garlands of leaves and berries.

The dials were white enamel with black or colored numerals, and the hands were pierced with elaborate and delicate designs. Beneath the dial the sunburst pendulum bob was visible.

Louis XVI

It is generally considered that the quality of workmanship and the artistry of design that were displayed in clocks produced during the second half of the eighteenth century represent the best by French clockmakers.

Louis XVI clocks were more symmetrical and less flamboyant than earlier styles. Wood cases were not entirely banished but the vast majority of cases was completely or partially ormolu work. Porcelain continued to enjoy a limited popularity but white marble became fashionable and was used either on its own or with applied ormolu panels and motifs.

Dials continued to be white enameled and small in diameter but dialmakers began decorating them with painted flowers and some exquisite pieces of work were produced.

Quite common during this period were marble or ormolu clocks in the shape of an urn or vase mounted on a marble base or stand. Side handles were frequently portrayed in the form of animal heads. The neck of the receptacle was covered by a tall lid the bottom half of which allowed the rotation of two horizontal chapter bands, one marked in hours and the other in minutes.

Coiled at the base of the neck was a snake with poised head and protruding tongue pointing to the time indicated on the

Figure 120. Louis XV cartel clock in a brass case decorated with festoons and pineapple finials. $1/2$-hour striking movement, white enamel dial and blue numerals, sunburst pendulum. Height 25 inches. Maker Ginbal, Paris.

175

Figure 121. Louis XV bronze bracket clock with brass mounts and finials surmounted by a bronze dog. 8-day movement with Dutch quarter strike. Height 18¹/₂ inches. Maker Francois Ageron, Paris.

Figure 122. Back of Francois Ageron's clock shown in Figure 121.

177

chapters.

Another popular clock was in the shape of a lyre which stood vertically on a circular moulded base. The case was usually either marble, decorated with ormolu work, or completely bronze. A mock gridiron pendulum was suspended from the top at the back to simulate the strings of the instrument and the movement escapement acted upon the bob instead of the pendulum rod.

Almost at the end of this period there appeared a type of clock that was reminiscent of Egyptian architecture. Two marble or bronze pillars or caryatides, mounted on a base of similar material, were used to support a portico beneath which hung the movement. Two vases or urns flanked the pillars and a pair of similar ornaments stood one at each end of the portico.

Directoire

During the four years of this period some excellent bureau clocks were made. They were usually of marble, very plain and almost devoid of curves in style, and were considered very fashionable when gracing a marble mantelpiece.

Empire

The pillar type clocks remained popular, some being made with four pillars instead of two.

There was a preponderance of cases in which it seemed the movement was added as an afterthought, such as a cart with the movement in a wheel, or a group of figures surrounding a rock with the movement in the rock face.

Colored onyx-marble, bronze, gilt and porcelain continued to be used but with a wider application. The majority of dials remained white enamel but many clocks were made with metal dials that were gilded or silver coated. Blue steel hands with pierced moon crests became very popular.

The quality of movements remained high but, with the exception of the bureau clocks, the design and workmanship of the cases did not match those of Louis XVI period.

Figure 123. Louis XVI lyre mantel clock. The surround is white marble enriched with ormolu work, and a ring of brilliants surround the white enamel dial. The clock stands on a red velvet plinth and is covered by a glass dome. Height 26 inches. Maker L. Leroy & Cie, Paris.

Figure 124. Empire cathedral bracket clock in mahogany with pierced brass panels and ormolu feet. 8-day movement with Dutch quarter strike and chime. Pendulum with silk suspension. Calendar dial. Height 17 inches.

Figure 125. 19th century ormolu and rouge marble clock set. Marble base beneath a pair of classical figures supporting a spherical marble clock case surmounted by Cupid. The striking movement has snake hands. The four branch candelabra companion pieces are decorated with a snake and rams heads.

181

Figure 126. 19th century white marble clock set decorated with applied ormolu beading and leaf designs. The 8-day striking clock is supported by two bronze cherubs and has a painted dial surmounted by an ormolu vase of flowers. The companion set is a pair of white marble urns surmounted by triple branch ormolu candelabra of rose design. Height of clock 20 inches. Maker Henry Gooche, Paris.

The styling of bureau clocks remained in good taste and they are today held in high esteem by connoisseurs. They were exceptionally well proportioned and the simplicity of their parallelism made them aesthetically pleasing.

The cases and dials were usually gilt or silver and the pierced moon hands were blue steel or gold. Polished machine turning was invariably the only form of decoration.

CHAPTER 10

Acquiring A Grandfather Clock

WHEN assessing the condition and value of a grandfather clock a purchaser must rely either on his own judgment, or recruit the service of an accredited dealer. It would be most unwise to make a purchase without subjecting the clock to some kind of inspection. For those who have had little or no experience in the world of antique furniture or who have a limited knowledge of the functions of a clock movement, the choosing of a grandfather clock is not easy.

Grandfather clocks are to be found in auction sale rooms and antique shops, and to a lesser extent they are advertised for sale by private individuals. Members of The National Association of Watch and Clock Collectors receive a monthly Mart in which all types of clocks are advertised.

Prices brought at auction sales are not necessarily indicative of commercial value. The selling price is controlled by the strength of the bidding and after the reserve price has been reached, the hammer will fall in favor of the highest bidder. This does not mean that one should not bid at an auction sale, quite the reverse. If a grandfather clock is on view prior to a sale it should be examined and its value assessed. One can then bid within the limit of one's budget and with due regard to the considered value of the clock.

A more realistic valuation is usually obtainable from a dealer in antiques, particularly if he specializes in horology and more so if he is a member of an horological society.

A clock obtained privately or from a sale room frequently results in the purchaser being responsible for transportation and setting up the clock, whereas a dealer will deliver and set up as part of the sale. He also has facilities for cleaning the movement and carrying out repairs if required.

The value of a grandfather clock will depend on its age, maker, condition, complicated work and design, and it is these factors that have to be considered when making an assessment.

Usually, the older the clock the greater is its value. If the name of the clockmaker is well known, particularly if he should rank among the most eminent of makers, this alone can impose a high price, even before condition and refinements have been taken into account. The most valuable of English grandfather clocks are those with walnut cases made in the late seventeenth century by Tompion, Knibb or Quare.

Rarely is it possible to date a grandfather clock exactly but it is not too difficult to assess its age within a few years. Reference to a list of clockmakers' names is usually the first line of inquiry; this establishes the era in which the clock was made. Such lists are to be found in the books marked with an asterisk in Appendix Two. The clock case and the movement must then be examined for specific details and if they are present, notes should be made of the years during which these details were in use. That period of time which is common to all the details can be said to be the period during which the clock was made. In this respect the dates at the end of Chapters Five and Eight will prove helpful.

It is not uncommon to find clocks that at some time in their life have had alterations made to provide an additional function, e.g., fitting a strike train to a timepiece. While it cannot be denied that such alteration increases the practical usefulness of the mechanical device, nevertheless it destroys much of its originality which in turn considerably reduces its value as an antique.

Additional refinements such as bolt-and-shutter, chime,

musical, and moon phase will always add to the value, and a clock with a duration of one month will have a greater appeal than an eight-day clock.

The choice of case is important and it is usually advisable to give consideration to the room in which the clock is to stand. It would be most disappointing to find that a newly acquired clock was too tall to be installed. This can easily happen with a clock that measures seven feet or more to the top of the uppermost finial and a room with a low beamed ceiling.

The clock will be an additional piece of furniture and as such it needs to harmonize with the room. A mahogany case would probably look out of place in a room furnished with oak. Similarly, a wide heavily built case decorated all over with marquetry standing with Hepplewhite or Sheraton style furniture might be considered out of place.

The Case

Almost all oak, walnut and mahogany cases were originally finished by many applications of linseed oil followed by persistent polishing with beeswax mixed with turpentine. After many years of exposure, wood treated in this way develops a surface film known as patina which adds luster to the waxed finish. Providing the surface is the original, it matters little if it has been neglected because patient and vigorous rubbing with a soft cloth and a good quality wax furniture polish will restore the wood to its original condition.

Frequently one comes across clocks that have been coated with varnish in the mistaken belief that the general appearance will be improved. Such clocks should be avoided because the only restorative treatment is to scrape off the varnish and start again. Doing this on a veneered and inlaid surface calls for the use of skilled hands.

Inspect the cabinet work for damage. Examine the veneer for peeling, blistering, and tearing at the edges. If these defects exist there is little that can be done to effect a repair but they must be taken into account when assessing the value of the clock.

A badly hanging trunk door or hood door is usually repairable. Frequently the screws are rusty and loose in the woodwork. Sometimes the timber is split on either side of the screw holes making it impossible to tighten the screws. Local application of a small quantity of wood glue will usually effect a permanent repair and then new screws will complete the job. If the hinges are badly worn or damaged there is no alternative to fitting replacement hinges, but make sure they match the originals, or are in keeping with the period in which the case was made.

Wood frets that are badly damaged or completely missing are not easy to replace.

Finials on the tops of hoods are vulnerable which makes them prone to accidental damage. Frequently some or all are missing completely, but there is a good chance that replacements can be obtained from one of the many firms that deal in antique clock case fittings.

Ebonized cases that have been decorated with Japanese lacquer are usually in poor condition, much of the lacquer having chipped or flaked off. Nothing can be done about this and the purchaser must decide whether or not he is prepared to accept the case as it is.

Check the seat board and its support for rigidity. There should be no wobble. If the timber is badly split or has received a severe attack from wood-worm, the fitting of a new seat board is advisable.

Examine the case inside and outside very thoroughly for signs of wood-worm. Many dealers and collectors of antique furniture consider the presence of these tiny holes add to the antiquity of the piece. This may well be so but it would be most inadvisable to install a piece of furniture in one's home if the article contained active wood-worm. Wherever the little holes can be seen look for the tell-tale powdered wood dust immediately beneath. If this is present then the clock case must be suspect.

Dials and Hands

Dials with missing spandrel ornaments should be avoided unless one is sure that a replacement ornament can be obtained. Dial plates in need of restoration can easily be resilvered and lacquered by a dialmaker who at the same time will renew the black wax in the chapters and the hour and minute rings.

Hands are finished blue steel, oil black and gilt, but if they are in poor condition they will spoil the appearance of the dial. Broken hands can be repaired by silver soldering if the pieces are available. This work can be carried out quite easily by a spectacle frame repairer. If the hands are missing or damaged beyond repair, replacements can be obtained from a firm who specializes in the making of period hands. If the originals are not available as patterns, the supplier will need to know the exact length of the hands, whether steel or gilt, the approximate age of the clock, and the size and shape of the center hole.

The Movement

The condition of the movement is very important. If it has been working with dry pivots over a prolonged period the pivot holes in the plates will almost certainly have worn. This applies particularly to the long duration clocks with their heavier weights. Ideally the movement should be cleaned and oiled, set in motion and checked for correct functioning. This is not possible when viewing a clock that is offered for sale. Wind the clock and if it is reluctant to function and there appears to be no obvious reason, the pivot holes should be inspected so far as one is able after removing the hood. Hold the wheel arbors between finger and thumb and move the pivots in their holes; this will indicate the amount of wear. If there is an appreciable sideways movement then the plates are in need of rebushing. This is work that a clock repairer is well able to undertake.

Transportation

1. Unlock the hood and remove by lifting up or sliding forward.
2. Remove the pendulum by holding the rod near the top and lifting the suspension spring up and backwards from the suspension cock. Lower the pendulum through the crutch and take it away through the trunk door.
3. Wind up the weights to within a few inches from the top.
4. Remove the weights, bring the two S-shaped hooks together and hang from them a small weight of about one pound to keep the lines taut and in position on the barrels.
5. Remove the movement and the seat board as one and transport it on a wooden stand or box.
6. Lay the clock on its back suitably padded against damage. If the clock is to be conveyed in a large furniture vehicle, as would be the case when moving a complete household, the clock can be stood upright on a cushion and made secure to the side of the vehicle with cord. Padding should be placed beneath the cord to prevent chafing to the corners of the trunk.

Setting Up

1. The base on which the clock is to stand must be firm and preferably level.
2. Position the clock against the wall and check that it is upright in both directions by holding a plumb line against the front and against one side of the case. A long length of sewing thread with a small metal object tied to one end will suffice. Adjust as necessary by placing pieces of cardboard or thin wood beneath the corners.
3. Secure the clock case to the wall. This is done by drilling two screw holes in the back of the case beneath the seat board, spaced well apart, and in positions easily reached by a screwdriver through the open trunk door. Drill and plug the wall and to it screw a length of wood the same thickness as that of the skirting board and about two in-

ches wide. Cut a length a little less than the width of the trunk so that the ends will not show. Secure the clock case to the wall board by means of roundhead woodscrews and flat washers.

A grandfather clock can be installed crosswise in a corner but it requires a wooden frame to be made in the shape of an isosceles triangle. The two equal sides that form the right angle are screwed to the walls, and the third and longest side is used to support the clock.

4. Check all pivots to see if they are adequately lubricated. A dry movement is not uncommon among grandfather clocks because, under the pull of the weight, the movement is capable of functioning even though the oil has dried out, but the rate of wear in the pivot holes is considerably accelerated. For instructions on oiling see Glossary of Terms, under Oiling.

5. Inspect the lines. If they are frayed they should be renewed. Cut off the old line and remove the knot from inside the barrel. Tie a knot at one end of the new line and pass the other end through the large hole in the end of the barrel and out through the small hole in the side. Continue passing the line until the knot reaches the small hole and is held. Take the line down through the elongated hole in the seat board, round the weight pulley and up through the small hole in the seat board. The line is then cut to length and knotted to prevent it being pulled through.

If this second hole is too large to prevent a knot from passing, it will be necessary to tie on the end of the line a suitable cross-piece such as a wooden peg or a nail. The practice of securing the outer end of a line to a hook in the under surface of the seat board is to be discouraged. In the event of the clock's is being overwound, causing the weight pulley to strike the hook, there is every possibility that a burr can be produced on the rim of the pulley which will eventually fray the line. The correct length of a line is that which allows the barrel surface to be filled and no more; any excess length is likely to run off the end. Pull downward on the line to give it tension while winding it onto the barrel.

The choice of line rests with the owner of the clock; it matters little whether gut or steel is used providing it is strong enough to hold the weight. It is usual to use gut for small weights and introduce steel for the large ones. Eight-day clocks invariably use gut, while clocks of greater duration are fitted with steel. A length of flexible three-ply wire rope with about forty strands of fine steel wire will make an excellent metal line. Heat it to a cherry red color over a flame in the area in which it is to be cut and allow it to cool slowly. This will considerably reduce any tendency for the wire to untwist after cutting.

6. Refit the movement. Check that the seat board rests on its supports without any wobble, and that the movement is secure to the seat board. If the movement is not secure it will affect the beat of the pendulum and may stop the clock. Fit the hood and make sure that the dial is close to the glass all round the edge and that there are no gaps visible when the hood door is closed.

7. Insert the pendulum through the open trunk door and guide the suspension spring up through the crutch and along the slit in the support cock. Pull gently downward to   locate the suspension spring in the cock.

8. Re-hang the weights. If there is a difference in their sizes the smallest weight is used for the time barrel which is on the right in a strike movement and in the center of a chime movement.

9. Wind the clock. If the movement is an early type fitted with an endless rope it is advisable to lift the weight with one hand while pulling down on the rope with the other. This will relieve the arbor of much of the loading during the time the weight is being raised. With an eight-day movement where winding is done with a key through the dial, it is advisable to watch the ascent of the weight to prevent overwinding and possible snapping of the line

should the pulley hit the under surface of the seat board.

10. Set the movement in motion by giving the pendulum a gentle push and then wait a minute or two for it to settle down and listen to the beat. If the ticking is regular no adjustment is required, but if it is irregular, indicating that the escapement is out of beat, the movement is likely to stop. Adjustment is carried out by altering the position of the pendulum crutch. Watch the bob and note the distance it travels either side of the vertical position. The crutch is then carefully bent towards the shorter distance. Another method is to bend the crutch towards the louder tick but in either case the amount of bending should be small.

   Set the clock in motion and wait a minute or two for it to settle into its new beat. If necessary, repeat the process until the sound of the escapement appears to be regular and the bob swings equidistant either side of the vertical position.

11. Check that the pendulum is swinging in a flat plane by observing from the side of the movement. The pendulum should remain parallel to the back of the case throughout its swing, but if its path of travel is slightly curved this may be caused by a bent suspension spring. Straightening the spring will put the matter right. Another cause of the pendulum's swinging out of line is the foot of the crutch not being square with the back of the case causing a sliding action between pendulum rod and crutch. This defect is sometimes introduced while bending the crutch to adjust the beat. Repositioning the foot of the crutch is all that is needed to rectify the fault.

12. Check the synchronization of the strike mechanism with the hands by turning the minute hand to the twelve o'clock position and observing that the hour hand corresponds with the number of strikes. If the striking is controlled by a locking plate it will most probably be out of phase; this is quickly remedied by raising the locking lever and releasing the mechanism to strike the next hour. This process is repeated until the strike corresponds with the last hour indicated by the hands.

191

CHAPTER 11

Some Famous Makers

The Worshipful Company of Clockmakers

During the sixteenth century French blacksmiths who had learned the art of clockmaking journeyed to London to make iron chamber clocks. Their skills were copied by English blacksmiths and by the end of the century clockmaking in England had become established.

In 1578 the Blacksmiths Company was incorporated in England to look after the interests of blacksmiths. When many of its members turned their hands to the manufacture of clocks the Blacksmiths Company extended its interests to include the new trade.

In 1544 The Master Clockmakers of Paris was incorporated, and the number of its members who went to London rapidly increased. In 1627 they asked that letters patent be granted so that they could continue their clockmaking in London on a more permanent basis. Such license would have resulted in English clockmakers being faced with serious competition and they felt that the Blacksmiths Company was insufficiently influential to safeguard their interests and that the time had come to form their own guild.

In 1630 a group of prominent London clockmakers and some Freemen of the Blacksmiths Company formed a committee and petitioned Charles I for a charter. The request was granted and in 1631 a Royal Charter was issued and The Worshipful Company of Clockmakers was formed in London, the men responsible being enrolled as Brothers. They had no building of their own and meetings were conducted in taverns.

The functions of the Company were to safeguard the interests of its members and those of the public, and to ensure adequate training of apprentices under proper supervision and without exploitation.

The Company had authority over clockmakers within a radius of ten miles of the City of London. It had power to introduce its own by-laws and the authority to ensure that they were carried out, by force if necessary. General control was also exercised over all clockmakers throughout the kingdom.

The first task of the Company was to secure the position of English clockmakers. It was made illegal for any foreigner to work in London as a clockmaker unless he was employed by a member of the Company. A law was introduced forbidding the importation of clocks and watches, and the Company had authority to inspect the cargoes of ships and the contents of warehouses. Any resistance to entry was met by force with police in attendance.

Improved working conditions were introduced and employers were required to conform to the new standards.

In the interest of the public, efforts were made to eliminate the possibility of inferior work being produced. The Company had authority to visit workshops and destroy any faulty or shoddy work, and power to impose fines on clockmakers contravening any of the Company by-laws. This right of search continued into the reign of William III until it was abolished in 1700.

New regulations were introduced governing the administration and training of apprentices. No clockmaker was allowed to employ an apprentice unless he, himself, was a member of The Worshipful Company of Clockmakers. The period of training had to be seven years, at the successful conclusion of which the trainee was admitted as a Freeman clockmaker. A further period of two years was then required to be spent in the workshop of his master or any other master as a journeyman, after which he was called upon by the Company to make a piece of work of their choosing which was referred to as a masterpiece. When the work was complete it was submitted to the Master and Wardens of the Company and if approved, the Freeman was registered as a Master clockmaker. It was from the ranks of the Master clockmakers that England produced their most eminent clockmakers.

English Clockmakers

EDWARD BARLOW (BOOTH) was born in Warrington, Lancashire in 1636, and his parents wanted him to have an ecclesiastic career. His original name was Edward Booth but after he had been ordained he assumed the name of his Benedictine godfather.

Barlow was a man of talent but not a great producer of clocks like some of his contemporaries. Much of his time was spent designing and improving horological instruments.

In 1676 he invented rack striking and the mechanism was introduced by Tompion almost immediately. Tompion subsequently fitted rack striking to all his clocks and the same method of strike control is still used universally today.

In 1686 he invented a form of repeater mechanism for use in clocks and watches, but his application for a patent was rejected on the grounds that Quare had antedated him by about six years.

Barlow died in 1716.

EDWARD EAST was born in 1602 in the village of Southill, Bedfordshire, about two miles from Tompion's birthplace. East was the son of a blacksmith and as a boy he often helped his father at the forge. At the age of sixteen he traveled to London and became apprenticed to Richard Rogers.

When the Company of Clockmakers was formed in 1631, East was one of the ten founder members. He took an active part in its proceedings and in 1645 was elected Master.

About 1633 he acquired premises in Fleet Street, London at the sign of The Musical Clock; it was here that he made some of his finest watches and clocks, including night bracket type clocks. He was appointed watchmaker to Charles I and subsequently to Charles II. His work was always to a high standard and is today highly prized among collectors and dealers.

Late in the seventeenth century it is believed he moved to other premises close to Temple Bar at the sign of the Sun.

East died in 1697 having lived ninety-five years.

JOHN ELLICOTT, born in London in 1706, was the most distinguished watch and clockmaker in the Ellicott family. His father, also John, was a fine watchmaker and was admitted to the Company of Clockmakers in 1696.

In 1728 John Ellicott started a business in Sweeting's Alley near the Royal Exchange. In 1838 the old Royal Exchange was destroyed by fire and Sweeting's Alley was never rebuilt.

John Ellicott serial numbered his watches and number 123 dates from about the time he set up in Sweeting's Alley. He was a maker of fine clocks and he also designed public clocks. He invented a compensating pendulum, but it was little used.

In 1738 he became a Fellow of the Royal Society, and was later appointed clockmaker to George II. He died in 1772 and his business was continued by his eldest son Edward.

FROMANTEEL. In the seventeenth century there lived in London a family of clockmakers of Dutch origin. The two most famous, John and the third successive Ahasuerus, were both admitted to the Company of Clockmakers in 1663.

John was apprenticed to Simon Bartram, Master of the Company of Clockmakers in 1646, while Ahasuerus was apprenticed to Thomas Loome, elected Brother of the Company of Clockmakers in 1649.

In 1657 John Fromanteel went to Holland to learn from Saloman Coster the principles of Christiaan Huygen's pendulum clock. When he returned to London a few months later, his family began making pendulum movements, as evidenced by the announcement that appeared in the journals Mercurius Politicus dated October 27th 1658, and Commonwealth Mercury dated November 25th 1658, which read as follows:

195

"There is lately a way found out for making of clocks that go exact and keep equaller time than any now made without this Regulator (examined and proved before His Highness the Lord Protector by such Doctors whose knowledge and learning is without exception) and are not subject to alter by change of weather, as others are, and may be made to go a week, a moneth, or a year, with once winding up, as well as those that are wound up every day, and keep time as well, and is very excellent for all House Clocks that go either with springs or weights; and also Steeple Clocks that are most subject to differ by change of weather. Made by Ahasuerus Fromanteel, who made the first that were in England. You may have them at his house on the Bankside, in Mosses Alley, Southwark, and at the sign of the Mermaid, in Lothbury, near Bartholomew lane end, London."

John made a number of fine grandfather clocks between 1660 and 1670 some of which are still in existence, and Ahasuerus produced some beautifully executed bracket clocks as well as grandfather clocks. Work by either of these two makers has today a very high value.

GEORGE GRAHAM was born among England's lakes in the county of Cumberland in 1673. At an early age he tramped his way to London, a distance of nearly three hundred miles, where in 1688 he became apprenticed to Henry Aske until 1695.

At the completion of his apprenticeship he was admitted a Freeman of the Company of Clockmakers and went to work for Thomas Tompion. The following year he married Tompion's niece Elizabeth.

A deep and lasting friendship developed between master and pupil and under Tompion's direction, Graham's skill and knowledge came to at least equal that of Tompion himself. During the latter part of Tompion's life Graham managed his uncle's affairs and during these last few years some clocks were engraved with both their names on the dial.

In 1713 Tompion died at the age of seventy-four leaving his business to his nephew and friend and for the next seven years Graham carried on at the Dial And Three Crowns. He became known as 'honest George Graham' and was well liked and respected for his kindness and generosity.

In 1715 he invented the dead-beat escapement which made a very valuable contribution towards achieving precise timekeeping.

Premises across the road from the Dial And Three Crowns became vacant in 1720 and Graham moved his business naming the new establishment Dial And One Crown. He became well known for his papers on horological matters and was highly respected for his skill in the making of mathematical instruments for the purpose of astronomical studies and observation. He was involved in the design of England's first planetarium. For his work in this field he was made a Fellow of the Royal Society in 1721, and the following year was elected Master of the Company of Clockmakers.

In 1726 he invented the mercury compensated pendulum and this, used in combination with his dead-beat escapement, produced an accuracy in timekeeping never before attained.

Graham continued Tompion's practice of numbering clocks, and he commenced at 600. Altogether he made 174 clocks and about 3000 watches.

In 1751 Graham died, and in recognition of his valuable contributions to science he was honored by being buried in Westminster Abbey. Tompion's grave was opened and Graham was laid to rest at the side of his friend. In death the two men were reunited.

JOHN HARRISON was born near Pontefract, Yorkshire in 1693 and when he was seven years of age his parents moved to Barrow in Lincolnshire. His father was a carpenter and John Harrison had been brought up to follow the same trade, but he had an aptitude for mechanical things and it was not long before he was taking an interest in clocks.

Harrison's ability as a clockmaker was the result of being

self taught. Because he had not served an apprenticeship he was ineligible for acceptance into the Company of Clockmakers. His earliest efforts in the field of horology were to clean and repair clocks. He then went on to make grandfather clock cases. In 1715 he completed two grandfather clocks, each with movements almost entirely of wood that produced remarkably accurate timekeeping. One of these clocks can be seen in the Science Museum, London. It is wound by a key, the holes for which are in the bottom corners of the dial and hidden by removable spandrel ornaments.

About 1726 Harrison produced three inventions. The first was the gridiron compensating pendulum that was designed to take advantage of the differing rates of expansion between steel and brass rods. The second was the grasshopper escapement. This was an arrangement similar in action to an anchor escapement except that the pallets were pivoted to the anchor and held in place by light spring pressure. The pallets were frequently made of lignum vitae. The third invention was another form of maintaining power, sometimes called Harrison's maintaining spring. When the pull of the weight turned the barrel, a spring was compressed against the main wheel causing the main wheel to rotate. When the barrel was turned in the reverse direction during winding, the spring pressure was retained by a ratchet and was sufficient to keep the time train going until winding was complete. This principle of maintaining power is in general use today in regulators.

By far the greatest of Harrison's achievements was the production of five marine timekeepers, a task to which he devoted more than half his life.

The Board of Longitude, appointed by the British Government, offered large sums of money to anyone who could design a marine timekeeper that would enable the crew of a ship at sea to calculate accurately their longitudinal position within specified limits.

Harrison's interest was aroused and in 1728 he journeyed to London bringing with him his gridiron pendulum, the

198

grasshopper escapement, and a set of drawings illustrating his ideas for a marine clock. Graham was asked to conduct a preliminary interview and his advice to Harrison was to return home and make a timekeeper so that it could be put to the test. Graham loaned him some money to help him with his project.

In 1735 Harrison returned to London and took up residence in Red Lion Square. He had brought his timekeeper with him which was a bulky affair in a wood frame. The movement was fitted with two balances and controlled by the gridiron compensated pendulum. The clock was inspected and tested over a period and it was the opinion of a committee of clockmakers that a certificate of worthiness should be given.

The following year Harrison sailed to Lisbon with his first marine clock on a King's ship. The clock was able to correct the ship's reckoning and when he returned to England he was paid £500 to continue his work.

In 1739 he completed his second clock and a year or two later he produced a third. In 1749 the Royal Society presented him with a gold medal for the best invention of the year.

About this time he began designing a fourth timekeeper. It was to be a more portable instrument in the form of a pocket watch. When it was finished he presented it to the Board of Longitude along with a request that it be taken and tested according to the terms of the Act. After considerable delay permission was finally given for him to sail with his watch to Jamaica. He sent his son William who sailed from Portsmouth in November 1761 on the 'Deptford', their first port of call being Madeira. After three days, Harrison's watch indicated that the ship was off course and although the Captain had faith in his own reckoning, William persuaded him to alter course. Late the following day they sighted Madeira.

The following January William Harrison sailed from Jamaica bound for England, and in the five months he had been away the watch showed an error of less than two minutes slow. This was well within the limits laid down by the Board which authorized that payment of £5000 was to be made to Harrison. The Government officials were not completely satisfied and wanted a further test carried out, but Harrison had more ideas for improvement and so he set to work and made another watch.

In 1764 William Harrison sailed to Barbados with his father's No. 5 timekeeper with almost uncanny results. William was away from England a little over twenty-two weeks and when he arrived back, the degree of accuracy extended beyond anyone's hopes. The Government immediately paid to Harrison another £5000 with the proviso that he must explain the workings to a committee. This he did and Kendall, a member of the committee, was elected to make a true copy of Harrison's chronometer, as it had come to be called.

In 1773 George III ordered that a final payment of £8750 should be made to Harrison.

The first four timekeepers, together with Kendall's copy, are in the National Maritime Museum, Greenwich, London, while his fifth is in the Guildhall Museum, London.

After his father's death William made a sixth marine timekeeper but its whereabouts is unknown.

John Harrison died in 1776 at the age of eighty-three and was buried at Hampstead Church, London.

KNIBB. This family of clockmakers lived in London during the second half of the seventeenth century. Samuel was admitted to the Company of Clockmakers in 1663, Joseph in 1670, Peter in 1677, Edward in 1700, Joseph (junior) in 1717. John, who was a younger brother of Joseph (senior) went with him to Oxford in 1667 and once away from London became ineligible for election to the Company.

Joseph (senior) became the most famous member of the family. Shortly after his arrival in Oxford he started a business and among his customers was Trinity College, for which he made clocks. This brought protests from other clockmakers in the city because Joseph was not a Freeman of Oxford. They demanded that he move away, but Trinity College put him on its payroll as a gardener which meant that he was safe. He was, however, made a Freeman in 1668.

In 1691, Joseph moved to London leaving behind his younger brother John, who became Mayor of Oxford in 1700. Joseph started a business at the sign of The Dyal in Serjeant's Inn, Fleet Street, and in 1697 moved to Suffolk Street, Charing Cross, at the sign of The Clock Dyal. He was well known for the high quality of his workmanship and the elegance of his clock cases.

Whereas other clockmakers changed their style according to fashion, Joseph preferred to retain traditional features. His bracket clock and grandfather clock dials continued to display narrow chapter rings and spade hour hands and many of his grandfather clock cases retained the same narrow appearance typical of the earliest clocks. It is, therefore, easy to make the mistake of thinking a clock by Joseph Knibb to be older than it is by its outward appearance.

He made a number of night clocks, examples of which have survived, and he also invented Roman striking. In recognition of his ability he was appointed clockmaker to Charles II and later to James II.

Joseph ended his days at Hanslope, Buckinghamshire, and clocks made during this period were inscribed "Joseph Knibb att Hanslop" or "Joseph Knibb of Hanslope" written in his typically flamboyant style. He died in 1712.

THOMAS MUDGE, son of a clergyman, was born in 1794 in Exeter, Devon, and became famous for his marine timekeepers, watches and regulators. At an early age he showed a distinct interest in mechanics and when he was sixteen his father put him to apprenticeship with George Graham in London.

Mudge showed great promise and under Graham's instruction quickly developed into a watch and clockmaker of unusual talent. On the completion of his training he was given a position of some responsibility in Graham's business, and in 1738 was admitted to the Company of Clockmakers.

Mudge remained in Graham's employ until his master died in 1751, and then went into business on his own.

His mastery of the art of watchmaking had long been established and he was asked by Ferdinand the Sixth of Spain to make a timekeeper of unique design. This he did in the form of a striking watch with repeat mechanism and equation work set in the head of a walking cane.

In 1755 he entered into partnership with William Dutton who also had been apprenticed to Graham. Together these two men produced watches of great elegance and accuracy.

In 1759 Mudge made horological history when he made a pocket watch for George III. It was the first watch that automatically compensated for changes in temperature, and it was the first watch to be fitted with Mudge's invention of the lever escapement. The watch is now in Windsor Castle and is still in going order.

Mudge had been making a study of the requirements of marine timekeepers, and in 1765 he wrote a paper on the subject.

In 1771 he left the running of the Fleet Street business to William Dutton and took up residence in Plymouth where he was able to pursue his nautical studies. Three years later he made his first marine chronometer and sent it to Greenwich Observatory for trial. Admiral Campbell took the timepiece on a voyage to Newfoundland and on his arrival back in England, reported that the chronometer readings had been satisfactory. As a result of this, the Board of Longitude (See Harrison) paid Mudge the sum of £500 requesting he continue with his research.

In the meantime, in 1776, Mudge was conferred with the honor of being appointed clockmaker to George III.

In 1779 he sent two more marine chronometers to Greenwich Observatory for trial. After years of indecision the Government finally decided in 1793 to pay Mudge a further £2500 for his work, but it was too late for him to enjoy. He died a few months later.

DANIEL QUARE was born in the county of Somerset in 1647 and brought up as a Quaker. He served his apprenticeship with a clockmaker and then went to London where, in 1671, he was admitted a Brother of the Company of Clockmakers. The same year he started a clockmaking business at St. Martins le Grand, London, and it was while at these premises he married into a wealthy and influential Quaker family.

The business was a success and Quare produced some very fine clocks. In 1680 he invented a repeater mechanism that he used in clocks and watches.

It was about this time that he vacated St. Martins le Grand to take up residence in Exchange Alley, London, under the sign of The Kings Arms.

In 1686 Edward Barlow invented a form of repeater mechanism and applied for a patent to safeguard his interests. However, the Company of Clockmakers submitted Barlow's application to the Privy Council with a recommendation that a patent should not be granted on the grounds that Quare had been producing clocks and watches with a similar mechanism for some years.

It was the opinion of James II that both men should submit to him a watch with their own repeater mechanism fitted. This they did. Quare's watch had a short pin projecting from the edge of the case near the pendant which when depressed sounded the hour and the quarter. Barlow's watch had two pins, one for the hour and the other for the quarter hour. The king showed a preference for Quare's watch.

Quare specialized in making grandfather clocks of long duration, many of which ran twelve months between winds. He also made equation clocks.

Near the end of the seventeenth century he experimented with barometric instruments and in 1695 he was granted a patent for a portable barometer.

In 1708 Quare was elected Master of the Company of Clockmakers. Shortly after George I took the throne, Quare was appointed clockmaker to the king, but he refused to take the Oath of Allegiance that was required by all persons entering the royal palace. The problem was overcome by permission being given to allow Quare to use the servants' entrance at the rear.

In later years Quare took on a partner. He was Stephen Horsman who had been in Quare's employ since the beginning of his apprenticeship in 1701. The business continued to flourish under the new name of Quare and Horsman.

Quare died in London in 1724.

THOMAS TOMPION was England's most famous clockmaker and is frequently referred to as the father of English clockmakers. He was born at Ickwell Green near the village of Northill in Bedfordshire in 1639. Tompion's father and grandfather had both been the village blacksmith in their time and Tompion grew up in the environment of a forge. The blacksmith's workshop still exists. It has become a building of historic interest and proudly displays a plaque in commemoration of Tompion. It is interesting to note that not two miles away, in the village of Southill, Edward East was born thirty-seven years earlier. He, too, had a blacksmith father and at an early age went to London to become one of England's greatest clockmakers. One wonders whether Tompion's success was partly due to some influence that East may have had.

Records are vague as to how Tompion spent his early life. It is known that he journeyed to London and he must have been befriended and given an apprenticeship by a clockmaker because in 1671 he was accepted as a Brother into The Company of Clockmakers.

In 1674 he took over the tenancy of premises at the corner of Fleet Street and Water Lane (now Whitefriars Street) where he started a business by the sign of The Dial and Three Crowns. He remained a bachelor but as time passed his household grew. He provided accommodation for relations, journeymen, apprentices and servants. Part of the premises were used as workshops and at the front was a shop where he sold clocks and watches. Among his relations was a niece who married Edward Banger, a clockmaker employed by Tompion.

Shortly after moving into the house in Water Lane, Tompion met Dr. Robert Hooke and a friendship developed.

Hooke was a scientist and mathematician and produced a never ending supply of new ideas, but he needed a man with creative skill to put his ideas into practice. Hooke was a man with influence and some of Tompion's work came to the attention of Charles II and the Astronomer Royal.

Hooke invented a form of spiral balance spring for use in pocket watches, and Tompion included Hooke's design in a watch which he presented to Charles II. It should be noted that Christiaan Huygens had also invented a spiral balance spring which was fitted to watches made in Paris.

In 1676 Tompion was asked to make the first clocks ever to be installed in Greenwich Observatory. He made two timepieces each with a duration of one year. In the same year he introduced rack striking, an invention of Dr. Edward Barlow, and included this new mechanism in all his later clocks.

In 1695 he designed the first equation clock. The additional mechanism necessitated increasing the height of the dial which he did by extending it in semi-circular fashion. This new dial became known as the break-arch or broken-arch dial. The clock was presented to William III and was later handed down through the Royal family and kept in Buckingham Palace where it is today.

The same year he engaged a new assistant, George Graham, fresh from apprenticeship. Graham was destined for great things and he became a lifelong friend of Tompion.

In 1701 Tompion took on Edward Banger as a partner but the relation lasted scarcely more than six years because in 1707 the partnership broke up.

Tompion's business grew and he became a man of wealth. It is not known how many clockmakers he employed, but it has been established that in his workshops he arranged the work in such a way that each man became a specialist in the making of certain components, which resulted in standardization and interchangeability of parts.

During his lifetime he was famous for his watches, but after his death it was for his clocks that he became better known. Records indicate that he must have made about 5500 watches and something like 650 clocks. About 1680 he started a system of giving each clock a number and it is known that these numbers go up to 542. Unfortunately they give no indication of the year of manufacture.

Tompion took little active part in the administration and functions of the Company of Clockmakers; he was more inclined to go his own way within the limits of the Company regulations. Nevertheless, in 1703, he was elected Master.

By this time Tompion had become the unchallenged leader among England's clockmakers and he was regarded in high esteem. In the world of horology he was a man of outstanding ability and some influence. Today he is famous the world over for his grandfather clocks and bracket clocks. Among his most ambitious pieces of work was a spring-driven, quarter-striking ebonized bracket clock of one year duration that was made for William III.

On the 20th November 1713 Tompion died and in recognition of his lifelong work he was buried in Westminster Abbey.

American Clockmakers

SILAS HOADLEY was born at Bethany, Connecticut in 1786. In 1800 he became apprenticed to his uncle who was a carpenter, and in 1807 he entered into partnership with Eli Terry and Seth Thomas making wooden grandfather clock movements at Greystone. These movements were sold complete with dial, hands, line and weights, and were hung on the wall without a case. They were frequently referred to as hang-up clocks. Owners had the choice of using them as they were, or having them fitted into tall cases. Many were in use a number of years before being cased which explains why so many old movements are found in cases of more recent manufacture.

In 1810 Terry left the company. Three years later Thomas also left and Hoadley carried on alone.

In 1849 Hoadley retired from the clockmaking business and occupied his time in local government and church activities. He died at Plymouth in 1870.

ELIAS INGRAHAM was born in Marlborough, Massachusetts in 1805. He served his apprenticeship as a cabinetmaker, and then in 1828, attracted by the growing clock industry, he moved to Bristol, Connecticut, where he worked as a clock casemaker.

He quickly became highly skilled and his work was in much demand. In 1831 he started his own clock business which is the E. Graham Company of today.

Ingraham specialized in designing clock cases. He was responsible for introducing the sharp gothic case but he did not protect it with a patent. It was extremely popular, so much so that it was eventually made, not only throughout North America, but in other countries.

Ingraham did not acquire great wealth as did some of his contemporaries but he did live to see his business become established and prosperous. He died in Bristol in 1885 at the age of eighty.

CHAUNCEY JEROME was born in Canaan, Connecticut in 1793, but when he was four years old the family moved to Plymouth, Connecticut. His father was a blacksmith.

In 1809 Jerome was apprenticed to a carpenter and on the completion of his indentures in 1816, he went to work for Eli Terry, making wooden cases for pillar and scroll clocks. Terry installed a circular saw in his factory, something quite new in those days, and taught young Jerome to use it. He was a willing pupil, eager to learn and it was not long before he had mastered the technique of making these shelf clock cases.

Jerome then decided to make a few clocks of his own. He bought some movements, made the cases, fitted them up and found a ready market that provided him with a good profit. This initial success encouraged him to continue and by 1821 he had made enough money to start a business of his own. He sold his house and moved to Bristol, Connecticut where he set up machinery not only to make the wooden cases, but also to cut wheel teeth so that he was able to speed up production of movements.

In 1825 Jerome introduced the bronzed looking-glass

clock and from then on the Terry pillar and scroll clock began to lose its popularity. The looking-glass clock was a success but even at the height of its production Jerome was one step ahead, thinking of his next venture. He wanted a small, inexpensive reliable clock with which he could flood the market and export to other countries. His idea was to produce thirty-hour clocks in such large quantities that the cost would be lower than ever before achieved. To do this he opened another factory in Bristol and between them many thousands of clocks were made.

In 1842 he exported clocks to England at such low prices that it caused a serious setback in the sale of English clocks. Shortly after this he exported to Europe and drove the Black Forest clocks from the market.

In 1844 he moved to New Haven and started a case factory, leaving the two factories at Bristol to concentrate on the manufacture of movements. The rate of output was higher than anyone had ever accomplished and then the following year disaster hit Jerome! One of his Bristol factories burned down destroying tens of thousands of movements. He immediately transferred the other Bristol factory to New Haven and tried to make good his losses.

About this time the clockmaking firm of Terry and Barnum Co. was insolvent and a merger was arranged with the Jerome Manufacturing Co. The arrangement was a failure from the beginning and by 1855 Jerome was financially ruined. He died in 1860.

ELI TERRY was born in East Windsor, Connecticut in 1772, and was apprenticed to Thomas Harland of Norwich, Connecticut, in 1786.

At the completion of his indentures in 1793 he started up a small business in Northbury (now Plymouth) making wooden clocks. The movements were individually made, using hand-powered cutting machines and Terry quickly realized that this old traditional method of production would never satisfy the rising demand for clocks.

In 1800 he moved to larger premises situated close to a

river. He diverted the flow of water and used the power to operate his machines. Here he made wooden movements for grandfather clocks and found that more clocks could be produced in a given time by mass production methods than had ever before been achieved.

In 1806 he sold the factory to his apprentice, Heman Clark, and bought a water-mill at Greystone, a village on the outskirts of Plymouth. The following year he contracted to manufacture four-thousand wooden thirty-hour movements complete with seconds pendulum, dial and hands, in three years. He engaged Seth Thomas and Silas Hoadley to assist him, and the first year was spent in setting up a production line and experimenting with different methods. The second year a thousand clocks were made, many of which were different because of continual changes in design. In the next year the remaining three thousand clocks were produced at a steady flow without further changes. Terry had proved to himself, and others who had thought his ideas scatter-brained, that not only were large quantities possible by mass production methods, but also the cost was considerably reduced.

In 1810 Terry sold his water-mill factory to Thomas and Hoadley and moved to Plymouth Hollow (now Thomaston), where he worked on an idea for an all wooden mantel clock.

In 1814 he invented the pillar and scroll clock which, to a great extent, replaced wall clocks. In 1816 he covered his invention by taking out a patent, but this in no way deterred other clockmakers from copying. The clocks were so popular, and the demand so great, that in no time it seemed everyone was making them.

By this time Terry's three sons, Eli (junior), Henry, and Silas Burnham, had joined their father who then traded under the name E. Terry & Sons.

Later, about 1824, Eli (junior) and Silas Burnham started their own factories in Plymouth.

By 1830 Terry was taking a less active part in the mass production of his clocks and was content to leave the management in the hands of his son Henry, while he turned his attention to the making of brass regulator clocks and turret clocks.

About 1839 sheet metal became available and very quickly clockmakers went over to the manufacture of metal movements and the pillar and scroll era came to an end.

Eli Terry died in 1852.

SETH THOMAS was born in Wolcott, Connecticut in 1785 and was apprenticed to a carpenter in 1799.

In 1807 he entered into partnership with Eli Terry and Silas Hoadley, manufacturing wooden grandfather clock movements at Terry's Greystone factory.

Eli Terry withdrew from the firm in 1810 and Thomas continued in partnership with Hoadley until 1813. Thomas then went into business on his own in Plymouth Hollow, and the following year started making Terry pillar and scroll clocks under license.

Thomas made excellent clocks and his business prospered. He was a rich man when he died in 1859.

SIMON WILLARD, the most famous of a long line of Willards who became clockmakers, was born in Grafton, Massachusetts, in 1753. He was one of twelve children, among whom Benjamin (1743-1803) and Aaron (1757-1844) also became famous for their clockmaking.

Simon produced mahogany eight-day grandfather clocks many of which were fitted with chime, calendar and moon phase mechanisms. There are some very fine grandfather clocks of one year duration, and astronomical clocks that he made still in existence.

In 1788 Simon Willard moved to Roxbury near Boston, and took up residence at the sign of the Clock Dial. He made thirty-hour timepieces, a variety of spring-driven clocks, chiming and musical clocks, but he was most famed for his invention of the banjo clock which he patented in 1802, and which remained popular for half a century.

Simon Willard's clocks provided him with a handsome income and he began to withdraw from the hustle and worry of industry and content himself with making clocks for public buildings. He made the turret clock for the University of Virginia at Charlottesville.

In 1848, at the age of ninety-five, he died in Boston, a prosperous man.

CHAPTER 12

Glossary of Terms

Acanthus - A prickly leaved plant.

Acorn Clock - An American spring-driven mantel clock that appeared about 1845, the shape of which resembled that of an acorn.

Act of Parliament Clock - Income tax in Great Britain was introduced by William Pitt during the reign of George III and, in 1797 Pitt levied an additional tax on clocks and watches. The Act read:

> For and upon Every Clock or Timepiece by whatever name the same shall be called which shall be used for the purpose of a clock and placed in or upon any dwelling-house or any office or building thereto belonging, or any other building whatever, whether private or public, belonging to any person or persons or Company of Persons or any Body Corporate or Politick or Collegiate or which shall be kept and used by any Person or Persons in Great Britain, there shall be charged an annual duty of Five Shillings.

> The Act went on to say that the annual tax on gold pocket watches was to be ten shillings and for those made of silver or non-precious metals it would be two shillings and sixpence. The Act also included makers and sellers of clocks and watches. Those whose business premises

212

were in London would pay a tax of two shillings and six-pence; others who earned their livelihood in the provinces would pay one shilling.

In those days such sums of money represented a high percentage of a man's income and the majority of people could not or would not pay the tax. Many disposed of their clocks and watches, and makers and shopkeepers went out of business. A great number of men found themselves without employment and the situation became so serious that after twelve months the tax was repealed.

In the meantime, tavern landlords and innkeepers ordered large timepieces to be made which were hung in their premises for the benefit of customers, and it was these clocks that became known as Act of Parliament clocks.

The weight-driven movements were controlled by one seconds pendulums and fitted into round wooden cases with a short narrow trunk beneath. The dials were made of wood and painted black with gilt numerals and minute divisions. Roman numerals were used inside the minute band to mark the hour positions, while Arabic numerals were painted outside at every fifth division. The dial was fitted with a center seconds hand, and just below the center arbor was the hole to receive the winding key.

The trunks were usually lacquered and the doors were decorated, some in Japanese style while others displayed portraits in English settings.

After the tax was repealed the manufacture of these clocks continued to the middle of the nineteenth century but the black dials were discontinued in favor of white dials with black numerals.

Alarm - Sometimes spelled Alarum. A mechanical device which causes a hammer to strike rapidly against a bell at a predetermined hour. More usually found in lantern clocks.

Amplitude - The distance covered by the bob of a pendulum in a normal swing from one side to the other.

Anchor Escapement - This invention is generally attributed to Dr. Robert Hooke but believed to have been used first by William Clement of London about 1671. It requires very little angular movement for efficient operation, less than five degrees in fact, which means that the pendulum is also limited to the same small amount of movement. This has the advantage of being able to use a long pendulum with a one second rating, which gives greatly improved timekeeping, instead of the inferior half-second short bob pendulum.

The driving power in the train tries to turn the escape wheel in the direction indicated by the arrow in Fig. 127. Tooth (d) presses on the curved face of the entry pallet (f) and lifts it, causing the anchor to rock about its fulcrum.

The anchor is secured to an arbor which also carries a crutch, and therefore all three pieces must move together as an assembly. The crutch cannot move without taking

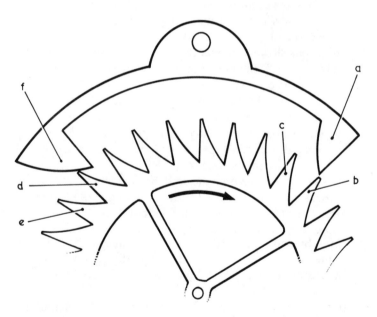

Figure 127. Anchor or recoil escapement. Solid pallet.

214

the pendulum rod with it and so when tooth (d) causes pallet (f) to lift, the pendulum must swing.

At the same time that pallet (f) is raised, pallet (a) is lowered in front of tooth (c). The anchor continues to rock until tooth (d) escapes and then the wheel rotates further until tooth (c) drops onto the curved face of pallet (a).

Before tooth (c) can exercise any influence over the anchor, the pendulum continues to swing in the original direction until its inertia is exhausted. This causes slight further lowering of pallet (a), the curved surface of which presses against tooth (c) and pushes the wheel backward giving it recoil. Tooth (c) then takes over and raises pallet (a) which causes the pendulum to swing in the reverse direction. When pallet (a) is high enough to permit tooth (c) to escape, tooth (e) will drop onto pallet (f) giving the pallet an impulse and the cycle begins again.

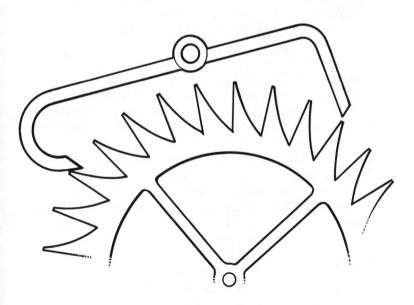

Figure 128. Anchor or recoil escapement. Strip pallet.

It is the slight reverse motion of the escape wheel each time a pallet drops that makes the anchor escapement a recoil escapement. This backward movement can often be seen on the seconds hand of a grandfather clock.

Fig. 128 shows a strip pallet anchor which is fitted to low-priced clocks. It is a strip of steel bent to the same angles as the solid pallet and functions in the same way, but it is cheaper to produce.

Arabesque - Curiously intertwined foliage and scrolls reminiscent of Arabian designs.

Arbor - A round steel spindle that carries a pinion, wheel, lever, hammer or anchor. The ends are reduced in diameter to form pivots which are supported in pivot holes drilled in the plates of the movement. The square or radiused collar formed by shaping the pivot serves to locate the arbor between the plates and the reduced diameter lowers the surface friction. The diameter of the arbors and pivots will vary according to the load under which they will have to function.

Arc - The angle, expressed in degrees, through which a pendulum moves in a normal swing from one side to the other.

Automata - Models or figures which are caused to move automatically at certain times by the action of time or strike wheel trains. Probably the most notable producers of this form of novelty were the German clockmakers of Nuremburg.

Back Plate - The two plates of a movement frame are known as the back plate and the front plate. That which is further from the dial is the back plate.

Balance - The energy stored in a wheel train after a clock has been wound is released in small measured amounts under the influence of a mass weight controller known as a balance. With medieval clocks this took the form of a foliot which consisted of an iron bar that swung horizontally, first in one direction and then the other, on a central pivot. Adjustment was effected by altering the position of a weight that hung from each arm. This form of balance was succeeded by an iron wheel.

Balloon Clock - A style of English bracket clock that appeared about 1760. The shape was not unlike that of a hot-air balloon from which it derived its name.

Banjo Clock - An American clock that was patented by Simon Willard in 1802. It was originally a hanging timepiece but because of its popularity, strike trains were subsequently added and some clocks were designed to stand. It is so named because of its similarity in shape to the musical instrument.

Baroque - A bold but sometimes odd form of decoration that prevailed during the reign of Louis XIV. It is similar to rococo but considered to be more debased in style.

Basket Top - A pierced silver or metal gilt decoration covering the wooden tops of some English bracket clocks during the latter part of the seventeenth century.

Beat - The 'tic-toc' of a pendulum timekeeper is the sound made by the escape wheel teeth hitting the pallets of the anchor at each swing of the pendulum. This is called the beat and the sound should be steady. If the clock is not in beat it will produce a long 'tic' and a short 'toc' indicating that the clock is not upright or that the pendulum crutch is in need of adjustment. Similarly, the ticking of a balance wheel escapement must be steady, otherwise the movement will stop.

Bell Top - The most popular shape of wooden top used on English bracket clocks.

Bezel - The metal ring that holds a clock or watch glass.

Bob - The weight on the end of a pendulum. Originally referred to the small round pear-shaped weight which was screwed onto the lower end of a half-seconds pendulum, known as a bob pendulum, fitted to lantern clocks with verge escapements and very early English bracket and grandfather clocks.

With the introduction of long pendulums the weights were larger and heavier. They were usually made of lead and cased in brass. A clear hole was drilled right through allowing them to slide over the thread at the bottom of the pendulum rod and their position was made adjustable by means of a rating nut beneath.

Bolt and Shutter - This was a simple device that provided maintaining power during winding. It was in use in England and was fitted to some very early grandfather clocks about 1660.

Between the movement plates was an arbor that projected forward of the front plate. Attached to the arbor were two levers, one between the plates and the other on the forward end. The inside lever carried a short length of thin flexible spring close to the teeth of the center wheel and was so positioned that by turning the arbor the spring engaged the wheel teeth.

The other lever was weighted and carried two shutters that slid behind the key winding holes in the dial. Attached to the forward lever was a cord that hung inside the case which, when pulled, raised the forward lever thus removing the shutters from the winding holes. At the same time, the inside lever was moved and the flexible spring became engaged with the center wheel teeth exerting sufficient pressure to keep the wheel train moving. This auxiliary power lasted two or three minutes which was ample time for normal winding.

After the key was withdrawn the bolt spring continued to follow the center wheel. At the same time the forward lever slowly fell under the influence of its own weight until finally it came to rest when the shutters returned to their position behind the winding holes. In this position the bolt spring was disengaged from the teeth of the center wheel.

Boulle - Charles Andre Boulle was a Frenchman, born in Paris in 1642, who became famous for his inlay work. His technique was to place, one on top of the other, two thin sheets of tortoise-shell and brass, and with a very fine saw cut out the shapes. The two materials were then fitted together; i.e., the brass shape would be fitted into the tortoise-shell sheet and vice versa.

The fitting of brass into shell was known as the 'first

part' and was more sought after than the inlay of shell into brass which was known as the 'second part'. The pieces were glued to an oak base and the surrounds veneered with ebony to complete the coverage. Most of Boulle's work was designed in baroque style or Arabesque.

When he died in 1732 his work was carried on by his sons and Boulle marquetry remained popular well into the eighteenth century.

Break Arch - Frequently called broken-arch. Some grandfather and bracket clock dials had an arched top, the diameter of which was less than the width of the dial plate. The tops of the cases were invariably shaped to match and these arches were known as break-arch.

Bronzed Looking Glass Clock - A style of American clock introduced by Chauncey Jerome in 1825.

Bulls Eye - A convex glass window in the trunk door of a grandfather clock through which the bob of the long pendulum could be observed. The originals were the centers of sheets of blown glass and were about half an inch thick in the middle.

Bush - When pivot holes in movement plates become badly worn, the arbors can no longer be located in their correct positions due to the excessive sideways movement of the pivots. This in turn affects the depthing of the wheels and the movement either functions badly or stops. The rate of wear is accelerated by lack of oil and is more pronounced in weight-driven clocks. The remedy is to disassemble the movement, enlarge the worn pivot holes by drilling, and hammer or press in brass bushes made for the purpose. These bushes are predrilled and when in position in the plates, the holes are broached to the size required for the pivot.

Calendar - The majority of grandfather clocks and early bracket clocks indicate the day of the month through a small square or rectangular aperture in the dial. The most usual arrangement has a wide flat brass ring which operates on rollers and is located behind the main dial.

This ring is called the calendar circle. It is silvered and engraved with Roman numerals from 1 to 31 on one face and is cut with thirty-one teeth around its inner edge. A toothed wheel is mounted on the hour wheel pipe and engaging with it is another wheel with twice the number of teeth. The first wheel rotates once in every twelve hours and therefore the larger wheel, which is called the calendar wheel, rotates once in every twenty-four hours. In the face of the calendar wheel is a pin that engages the teeth of the calendar ring and about midnight this pin pushes the calendar ring forward by one tooth and the next number appears in the dial aperture. At the end of a month containing less than thirty-one days the calendar circle has to be moved round to the numeral 1 by hand. This is accomplished with a thin pointed instrument.

Cannon Pinion - Sometimes referred to as the cannon wheel, it belongs to the motion work or dial wheels as they are frequently called. Part of the cannon pinion is a pipe that is squared at its forward end to carry the minute hand. The pipe fits snugly over the center arbor and is driven by it under the influence of a thin flat brass friction spring, the resistance of which is overcome by slight pressure when re-setting the hands.

Capital - The top part of a column.

Cartel Clock - A French wall clock of Louis XV period.

Caryatid - A female figure used instead of a column to support an entablature.

Center Seconds - A slender seconds hand pivoting at the center of the dial and reaching the minute divisions. Sometimes referred to as a sweep seconds hand.

Chamber Clock - This was the first domestic mechanical clock. It was made in Germany, France and Italy early in the sixteenth century and was almost entirely of iron.

Chapter - Roman or Arabic numerals marking the hour positions on a dial.

Chapter Ring - The circular band on a dial in which the numerals or chapters are engraved or painted.

Chase - The art of engraving on the outside of raised metal

work. Engraving in relief.

Chime-Silent Control - A manual control, usually situated in the break-arch dial of a grandfather or bracket clock, by which the chime can be silenced when required.

Circa or C. - About or around.

Clepsydra - An Egyptian water-clock in use about 1400 B.C.

Clickwork - See Ratchet.

Clock - See Timekeeper.

Coffin Clock - The very first grandfather clocks. So named because of their resemblance to a coffin.

Complicated Work - Mechanisms that are additional to time-keeping and striking, such as chime, calendar and astro-nomical.

Count Wheel - See Locking Plate.

Crown Wheel Escapement - See Verge Escapement.

Crutch - This is a length of soft iron wire attached at one end to the anchor arbor, while the other end is shaped, usually in the form of a fork, to embrace the pendulum rod closely. With each impulse of the escape wheel against the pallets of the anchor, the crutch is caused to swing taking with it the pendulum. This allows the pendulum to be suspended independently of the escapement. There is no crutch with a verge escapement where the bob pendulum is secured to the end of the verge. The crutch was first used by Huygens about 1657.

Dead Beat Escapement - This was one of George Graham's inventions and it first appeared at the beginning of the eighteenth century. The principle of operation is almost identical to the anchor escapement but the shape of the mating faces on the pallets and the teeth of the escape wheel are such that there is no recoil action. Fig. 129.

In its original form the pallets of this escapement span-ned fifteen teeth of the escape wheel. This was later reduced to ten teeth which proved very successful when used in regulators and with weight-driven movements having a one seconds pendulum. It is only in recent years that clocks in any quantity have been made with escapements having eight teeth embraced by the pallets.

221

The escapement requires the pendulum to be in good beat and the operating faces must be clean and free from gummy oil. If these two precautions are observed, then this escapement is capable of greater timekeeping accuracy than the anchor escapement.

Dial Pillars - These are the pillars in a plate frame movement that hold the dial to the front plate. Usually there are four but occasionally only three are used. Each pillar is riveted at one end to the dial plate, while the other end passes through a hole in the front plate and is held by a taper pin passing through the pillar behind the front plate. The length of the pillars is kept to a minimum allowing just sufficient clearance between the dial and the front plate to accommodate the dial wheels and strike mechanism.

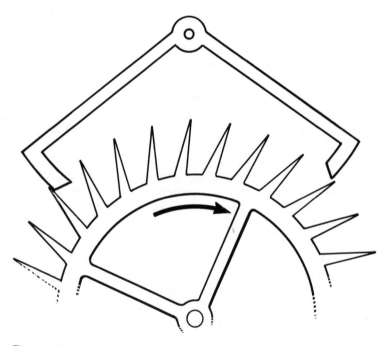

Figure 129. Dead beat or Graham escapement.

Dial Wheels - See Motion Work.

Dutch Striking - A form of striking introduced in England late in the seventeenth century involving the use of two bells of different pitch. The bell with the lower tone was used to sound the hour, while the other bell with the higher tone struck the following hour at the half hour.

Endless Rope - This is a form of maintaining power invented by Huygens about 1671 and was used in many English lantern clocks.

Equation of Time - The amount of time in minutes and seconds that must be added to or subtracted from solar time to give mean time.

Escapement - See Movement.

False Pendulum - See Mock Pendulum.

Finial - A bunch of foliage or other decoration on the top of a pinnacle, gable or spire. A popular form of ornamentation on the hoods of grandfather clocks.

Foliot - See Balance.

Front Plate - See Plates.

Fusee - A device sometimes fitted to a spring-driven movement to compensate for a progressive reduction of energy as the spring unwinds. It ensures a constant torque is applied to the wheel train at all times. See Reversed Fusee.

Gilding - The original process was known in England as water gilding, sometimes referred to as mercurial gilding, and in France where it was used extensively by makers of metal clock cases, it was called ormolu. The process involved the article to be gilded being rubbed over with a solution of subnitrate of mercury. An amalgam of mercury and gold was then applied which immediately attached itself to the pre-treated surface. The article was then heated over a charcoal fire until the color of the amalgam changed to dull yellow, and the gilded surface was then polished, burnished, washed and dried. The fumes given off during this process are extremely poisonous and few men today will undertake the work; it is, therefore, unlikely that such gilding would be renewed.

Water gilding produced a very durable surface and where tarnishing has taken place on an old clock the gilt will frequently respond to cleaning with soap and warm water. If more severe measures are needed the pieces must be removed and immersed for a few seconds in a solution consisting of one ounce of cyanide of potassium, one ounce of lump ammonia and half a pint of water. Remove the article and plunge it immediately in hot water and rinse it well.

While the fumes given off during this cleaning process are less noxious than those experienced from water gilding, they are nevertheless of a poisonous nature and the process is therefore best left to an experienced plater or renovator of antiques.

Gnomon - The pin of a sundial whose shadow points to the hour.

Going Barrel - A cylindrical brass drum, with main wheel attached, that contains the spring of a spring-driven timekeeper. This type of barrel is used without a fusee, and is mounted on a square-ended winding arbor.

Grande Sonnerie - The striking of the previous hour immediately before each quarter chime.

Grandfather Clock - The colloquial name for longcase clocks, known equally as tall clocks and tall-case clocks.

Grandmother Clock - A miniature version of the grandfather clock.

Gut - See Line.

Harrison's Maintaining Spring - The modern method of maintaining power invented by John Harrison and generally used with clocks fitted with dead-beat escapements after the bolt-and-shutter method fell into disuse. The barrel compressed a spring that drove the main wheel. When the barrel reversed during winding the spring continued turning the main wheel.

Hour Glass - See Sand Glass.

Jack - A figure on the outside of a clock that strikes a bell at each hour. Very popular in Europe and England during medieval times and still used on some public clocks.

Japanning - The Japanese art of applying lacquer to wood to produce colored designs and pictures for the purpose of decoration.

Journeyman - One whose apprenticeship to a clockmaker was complete.

Lancet Clock - A variant of the English bracket clock in the early nineteenth century that took the form of a Gothic lancet window.

Lines - The weights of thirty-hour movements were suspended by ropes that operated in spiked pulleys, but those of eight-day movements, and of greater duration, were hung from lines of stranded wire or gut wound round a barrel.

Line Barrel - A cylindrical brass drum onto which the gut or wire line of a weight-driven timekeeper is wound. The drums are sometimes grooved to receive the line whereas others are left smooth. Integral with the strike barrel is the great wheel, and with the time barrel is the main wheel. Each barrel is mounted on an arbor the forward end of which is squared to receive a winding key.

Locking Plate - Sometimes called a count wheel. Probably the oldest device used in striking clocks for controlling the number of hammer blows struck each hour. It is a metal disc that forms part of the striking train and has eleven notches cut in its periphery into which drops the hooked end of a lever. When the clock is ready to strike, the lever is raised and the disc slowly rotates. With each hammer blow the lever drops onto the land between the two adjacent notches. This process continues until the next notch comes into line and the lever drops into place and the strike mechanism is halted. The notches are spaced unequally and each land is longer than its forerunner thus allowing an additional hammer blow.

Lyre Clock - A French mantel clock of Louis XVI period shaped in the form of a lyre. Usually made of marble with applied ormolu, or completely bronze.

Maintaining Power - During the time a clock is being wound the motive power from the weight or spring is temporarily removed from the time train and the clock will stop. The exception to this is a spring-wound clock without a fusee which employs a going barrel. In this instance the motive power is not affected by the action of winding.

A number of devices have been invented to overcome this problem, the first of which was known as the bolt-and-shutter. Christiaan Huygens invented a method which was called the endless rope, and a third method was developed by John Harrison and known as Harrison's maintaining spring.

Marquetry - A form of decoration applied to a wooden base. The inlay of pieces of different colored woods to produce a variety of patterns and designs both geometric and pictorial.

Mean Time - The result of dividing a solar year into equal periods of time. All general use clocks indicate mean time.

Medieval - See Middle Ages.

Mercurial Gilding - See Gilding.

Meridian - Midday. When the sun is at its highest point.

Middle Ages - The period from the fifth century to the fifteenth century. Anything relating to that period is said to be medieval.

Mock Pendulum - Sometimes called false pendulum. It is a miniature pendulum positioned close behind a curved slot in the dial and kept in motion by the clock pendulum. It serves as a visual indication that the movement is functioning and was frequently fitted to bracket clocks.

Moon Dial - A popular subsidiary dial fitted in the break-arch of a grandfather clock dial. A slowly rotating disc behind an aperture in the dial plate indicated the age and phase of the moon.

Motion Work - The cannon wheel, minute wheel and hour wheel comprise the motion work, but when being considered together with calendar wheels they are all more generally known as dial wheels.

Motive Power - See Movement.

Movement - A timepiece is a device that indicates time by visible means only, but a device that indicates time by audible means as well as visual means is known as a clock.

A simple mechanical timepiece consists of a train of gear wheels for driving the hands with a source of power at one end and a controlling device at the other end. Fig. 130 illustrates a typical train. In America the gears that drive the hands are referred to as the time train whereas in Great Britain the term going train is used.

The source of power, known as motive power, is a

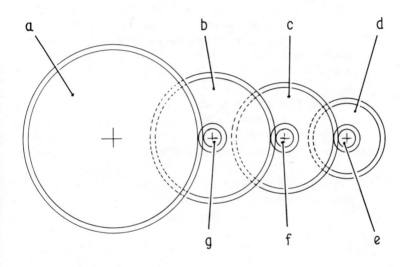

Figure 130. Typical 8-day time train.
(a) Drum (spring or weight) and great wheel. Rotates once in 12 hours.
(b) Center wheel. Rotates once in 1 hour. Carries minute hand.
(c) Third wheel.
(d) Escape wheel. Rotates once in 1 minute. Carries seconds hand.
(e) Escape wheel pinion.
(f) Third wheel pinion.
(g) Center wheel pinion.

hanging weight or a coiled spring that transfers its energy to the wheel train through a ratchet. At the other end of the train is an escapement that prevents the wheels from rotating at high speed by placing an obstruction in the path of the last wheel. This wheel, which is called the escape wheel, is released one tooth at a time, and so all wheels are allowed to rotate in a series of small measured distances.

In the first mechanical clocks the frequency at which these teeth were released was controlled by a foliot and later by a balance wheel but these methods produced results which were far from accurate. It was not until 1657 when Christiaan Huygens invented the pendulum that any real improvement in timekeeping was achieved.

Similarly strike and chime mechanisms have their own wheel trains and their own independent sources of motive power, but they rely on the time train to set them in motion.

Music-Silent Control - A manual control, usually situated in the break-arch dial of a grandfather or bracket clock, by which the tune or melody can be selected or silenced.

O.G. Case - A wooden clock case rather like a heavy picture frame made from ogee section. This was the style used by Chauncey Jerome for his one-day brass movement clocks that he shipped to England in 1842 and which marked the beginning of America's export trade of clocks.

Ogee - A moulding S-shaped in section.

Oiling - A clock movement is not difficult to oil; the important things to know are where to put it and how much to apply. More harm can often be done by over oiling than by leaving the movement to run dry.

The teeth of wheels should never be oiled. Minute particles of abrasive matter floating in the air would settle in the oil and embed themselves in the soft brass. These particles are harder than the steel from which the pinions are made and it would not be long before there were signs of wear on the pinion leaves.

All pivots are lubricated and to this end the pivot holes

228

in the movement plates are countersunk on the outside faces of the plates. These are known as oil sinks and it is here that the oil is applied.

It is assumed the movement is reasonably clean. A dirty movement will have a residue or sludge in the pivot holes. The addition of oil will dilute it for a short period and then the oil will dry out and the movement will return to its former condition. A dirty movement has to be removed from its case, disassembled, cleaned, assembled and refitted. Instructions for this are contained in *Handbook of Watch and Clock Repairs* by this author.

Clock oil is supplied in small bottles and is sufficient to lubricate a large number of movements. It is a mixture of animal, vegetable and mineral oils that have been selected for their purity and low viscosity and which have been subjected to special refining processes. Genuine clock oil is available from any clock and watch materials dealer. Never use any other lubricant as it will be too gummy.

The method of application is to use an oiler. Take a length of stout brass, copper or steel wire about six inches long and bend it at one end into a circle to produce a handle. The other end is tapped with a hammer to form a spade shape. Use the oiler to transfer one or two drops of oil onto a piece of glass. Wipe the oiler dry and touch the end to the oil. A small quantity will be lifted which can be transferred to an oil sink by touching it with the oiler. Capillary attraction will cause the oil to flow. Treat all pivots in the same way.

Onyx - A beautiful variegated mineral frequently used for making cameos.

Ormolu - An alloy of copper, zinc and sometimes tin, used in gilding or bronzing French metal clock cases.

Patina - A film that develops on waxed wood after long exposure.

Pediment Top - An architectural style that was used for the tops of clock cases. It is triangular in shape and reminiscent of ancient Greece.

Pendulum - Until the middle of the seventeenth century the methods of controlling the release of energy in the time train of a clock were by foliot or balance wheel. Rarely were they capable of keeping time to within five minutes each day.

Then, in 1657, Christiaan Huygens applied the known principles of a pendulum to a clock movement with remarkably good timekeeping results. London clockmakers were the first to take up this idea commercially and they fixed the pendulum to the end of the verge in their lantern clocks. It was not until the introduction of the anchor escapement in 1671 that pendulums were independently suspended and linked to the escapement through a crutch.

Pilaster - A square column partly built into a wall.

Pillar Frame - Two horizontal flat brass plates are supported, one above the other, by four corner posts. Between the plates are narrow brass strips placed vertically one behind the other and drilled to take the arbor pivots. This type of frame was used in lantern clocks.

Pillar and Scroll Clock - A low-priced American clock with a thirty-hour wooden movement introduced in 1814 by Eli Terry who manufactured many thousands by his mass production methods.

Pinion - A toothed wheel of steel or iron with less than twenty teeth. Originally they were filed to shape, but early in the eighteenth century it was discovered that if iron wire was pulled through a steel drawer plate with a hole shaped to the profile of the pinion, the wire was transformed into a continuous pinion that could be cut to any desired length. This was known as pinion wire. The position of the pinion was then marked and the remaining length was reduced in diameter to form the arbor.

Another method of making pinions was to insert lengths of wire between two steel discs that were drilled at regular intervals close to the edge.

Pivot - The reduced diameter at the ends of an arbor that are supported in pivot holes drilled in movement plates.

Plate Frame - This type of frame superseded the pillar frame about 1660 in England. It consists of two brass plates, drilled with pivot holes, placed vertically one behind the other and separated by corner posts. This arrangement allows the time and strike trains to be placed side by side instead of behind each other, as was the case with pillar frames and so makes it possible to wind the clock from the front by means of a key inserted through holes in the dial. The plate immediately behind the dial is the front plate and that further from the dial is the back plate.

Pulleys - The trains of early thirty-hour weight-driven movements, such as were fitted to lantern clocks, were driven by spiked pulleys around which passed ropes or chains with a weight at each end. Pulleys intended for ropes were curved at the bottom of the flanges whereas those that were designed for chains had a square recess to accommodate the chain links.

Clocks of greater duration were driven by gut or wire lines wound round barrels and they had no need for driving pulleys. The weights of a thirty-hour clock were hooked directly to the end of the rope or chain, but those of an eight-day movement were suspended by hooks attached to pulleys around which passed the line.

Pull Quarter Repeat - A repeat mechanism which was set in motion by pulling a cord at the side of the clock. A lever was raised which released the strike and the last hour followed by the last quarter was struck. Fitted to some bracket clocks and intended for use by the bedside during the hours of darkness.

Quarter Chime - A clock that strikes three or more bells at each quarter.

Quarter Rack - The rack that selects which bells are to be used when striking each quarter.

Quarter Strike - A clock that strikes the quarters on less than three bells.

Rack Striking - This is a strike mechanism that is linked to the hands and which is put in motion by a pin on the minute wheel. The selection of hammer blows required

231

to be made at each hour is by means of a rack. A detailed description of the function of this strike mechanism will be found in Chapter Five.

Ratchet - When a clock is in need of winding it becomes necessary to have a means of breaking into the chain of moving parts so that one of them can be turned in reverse to wind up the weight or spring. This facility is provided by fitting a ratchet to the barrel (or driving pulley if the clock has a thirty-hour weight-driven movement). A ratchet comprises a spring-loaded click that engages with a set of teeth. When turned in the direction of winding the click rides the teeth against the tension of the click spring, but when winding is finished the click engages the teeth and transmits the motive power to the train of wheels.

Recoil Escapement - See Anchor Escapement.

Regulator - A tall-case weight-driven pendulum timepiece without strike mechanism or complicated work. The movement is accurate; it is fitted with a dead-beat escapement and a compensated pendulum. It is a precision timepiece without refinements and was not intended for domestic use. They are frequently to be found in the workshops of clock repairers who use them as standards, or laboratories where precise time is a requirement.

Reversed Fusee - Serves the same basic function of a fusee but is so made that the chain has to cross over resulting in the fusee and the spring barrel rotating in opposite directions.

Rise and Fall - An arrangement whereby the effective length of a pendulum could be reduced or increased by raising or lowering the suspension from the front by means of a manually operated pointer on the dial.

Rococo - Style of furniture decoration popular during the reign of Louis XV. Grotesque designs including unsymmetrical scrolls, broken curves, shells, and a multiplicity of tasteless detail. To be found on many eighteenth century French clocks.

Roman Striking - An abbreviated form of striking designed to

232

reduce the number of hammer blows needed, thereby extending the period between windings. See Chapter Five.

Royal Pendulum - The name given to long pendulums, used in conjunction with anchor escapements in recognition of the patronage of Charles II.

Sand Glass - A tubular glass container closed at each end and waisted in the middle to form a restriction. In the container was a quantity of fine dry sand and when the container was stood on end the sand trickled from the upper bulb into the lower bulb in a predetermined time. They were made in different sizes to measure periods ranging from a few minutes up to four hours.

Shadow Clock - A primitive device that relied on the sun's casting a shadow of a cross-piece mounted above a board placed east-west and which was marked to indicate measured periods during the day.

Sheep's Head - A lantern clock with an enlarged chapter ring that extended beyond the sides of the movement frame and which resembled the appearance of a sheep's head.

Single Rope - Fig. 131. The most simple arrangement is shown at (a). Here the weight hangs directly from the drum and the clock will function so long as the weight continues to fall. The length of the rope, therefore, controls how long the clock will function before rewinding is necessary.

The arrangement at (b) introduces a pulley which is frequently secured at the top of the case. This has the effect of increasing the distance the weight has to travel to reach the floor and therefore the running time of the clock is increased.

A further improvement is obtained by using the arrangement as at (c). The free end of the rope is attached to the top of the case and a pulley is fastened to the weight. The rate of fall of the weight is halved; in other words the weight takes twice as long to reach the floor, but twice as much rope is required. Unlike arrangements (a) and (b) that had only one point of suspension for the weight, arrangement (c) has two

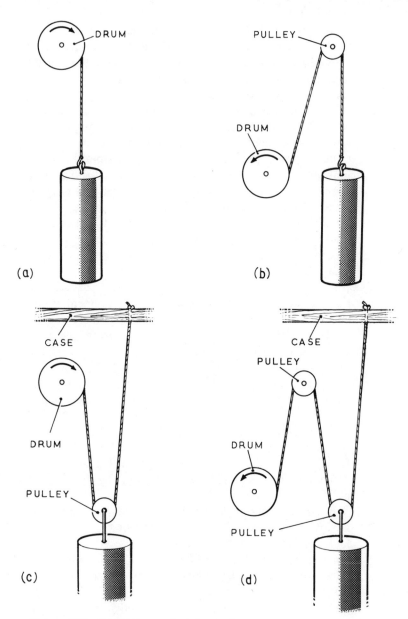

Figure 131. Single rope arrangements.

234

suspension points: i.e., the top of the case and the drum. This means that the pull of the weight is shared equally by these two points and now only half is available to drive the clock. To overcome this the weight must be doubled.

In the last arrangement (d) a pulley has been added to increase further the length of rope and thereby increase the running time of the clock at one winding.

Skeleton Dial - A dial that has been pierced so that the numerals are in silhouette. The centers of these dials are frequently treated in the same way to produce pictorial scenes.

Solar Time - The time indicated on a sundial according to the position of the sun in the sky. Sometimes referred to as apparent or true time. A solar day commences when the sun leaves the meridian and ends when the sun returns to the same position, but the time taken to complete the cycle is different each day.

Spandrel - The space between the curve of a chapter ring and the corner of a square dial plate.

Spandrel Ornament - The applied or engraved ornamentation that fills the spandrel.

Spring Barrel - A cylindrical brass drum without a wheel that contains the spring of a spring-driven timekeeper, and which is used with a fusee. It is the fusee that is mounted on the winding arbor.

Strike Silent Control - A manual control, usually situated in the break-arch dial of a grandfather or bracket clock, by which the strike mechanism can be silenced when required.

Sunburst - A design of pendulum bob fitted to French clocks during the period of Louis XV, and giving the appearance of the sun's rays.

Sundial - A device for telling the solar time by means of the sun's casting a shadow of a gnomon onto a graduated plate or base. Some were scratched in a vertical wall; others consisted of a marked plate or base laid horizontally on top of a low pedestal. There were also portable sundials, some small enough to be carried on the person.

Sweep Seconds - See Center Seconds.

Tabernacle Clock - Miniature tower clocks. See Figs. 14, 15, 16, 17.

Tall Case Clock - See Grandfather Clock.

Tall Clock - See Grandfather Clock.

Tavern Clock - See Act of Parliament Clock.

Thirteen Piece Dial - A distinctive type of French dial popular during the time of Louis XV. Each black Roman numeral was painted on a white enamel plaque that was applied to the dial plate. The thirteenth piece was a white enamel disc placed in the center of the dial plate. The small spaces betwen the thirteen pieces were filled with gilt ornamentation.

Tic Tac Escapement - A rare form of anchor escapement where the anchor was so shaped as to embrace only two teeth of the escape wheel instead of the usual seven. It was an unsuccessful attempt at retaining the advantages of a conventional anchor escapement while reducing its sensitivity to poise and thereby making it suitable for use in portable clocks such as bracket-clocks.

Timekeeper - A term that includes timepieces and clocks. A timepiece has a time train only, whereas a clock has time and strike trains. It is, however, common practice to refer to them both as clocks.

Timepiece - See Timekeeper.

Ting Tang Strike - The earliest known form of quarter-striking. Two bells of different tones are used, each being struck once for the first quarter, twice for the second and so on. It is said that the name is derived from the sound made by the large bells of public clocks in use during the Middle Ages.

Train - A line of wheels and pinions of calculated gear ratio, so arranged that they transmit motive power from one to the other terminating at the escapement.

Turret Clock or Tower Clock - A large clock, usually positioned high in a public building, whose dials are located at a distance from the movement. The hands are driven by horizontal leading-off rods.

Up and Down Dial - A subsidiary dial and hand, usually positioned at the top of a bracket clock break-arch dial, that indicates how far the spring has unwound.

Verge Escapement - Sometimes known as a crown wheel escapement, it is the oldest form of clock escapement. It was used, in conjunction with a foliot balance, on the earliest known weight-driven public clocks and was still being used in some clocks up to the late nineteenth century. Details of its function are given in Chapter Two.

Vernis Martin - An imitation Japanese lacquer finish used on some French clocks during the time of Louis XV.

Wagon Spring - An American invention that provided a clock movement with spring motive power without the need for a compensating fusee. Details of its function are given in Chapter Eight.

Warning - In modern trains the clock prepares itself to strike a few minutes ahead of the hour, and then waits for the train to be released exactly on the hour. This is known as the warning and the object is to ensure that striking takes place precisely when the minute hand points to twelve. Before the adoption of minute hands this degree of precision was unnecessary and in many early clocks the strike was set in motion in one action without any preliminary warning.

Water Clock - See Clepsydra.

Water Gilding - See Gilding.

APPENDIX 1

Bibliography

Books

*Baillie, G.H. - Britten's Old Clocks and Watches and Their Makers 8th edition. 1973.

*Moore, N. Hudson - The Old Clock Book. 1911.

*Dreppard, Carl W. - American Clocks and Clockmakers. 1958.

*Baillie, G.H. - Watchmakers and Clockmakers of the World. 2nd edition. 1947.

*Wenham, Edward - Old Clocks for Modern Use. 1951.

Cescinsky, H. & Webster, M.R. - English Domestic Clocks. 1913.

Willard, John Ware - A History of Simon Willard, Clockmaker. 1911.

Jerome, Chauncey - History of the American Clock Business. 1860.

Hoopes, Penrose - Connecticut Clockmakers of the Eighteenth Century.

Chandlee, Edward E. - Six Quaker Clockmakers. 1943.

Player, J.W. - Britten's Watch and Clock Makers' Handbook Dictionary and Guide. 15th edition. 1955.

In addition, this author, H.G. Harris, has written two books, Handbook of Watch and Clock Repairs (Revised Edition 1972) and Advanced Watch and Clock Repair, (1973) published by Emerson Books, Inc., Buchanan, N.Y. 10511.

*These books include a list of makers.

Journals

Bulletin of the National Association of Watch and Clock Collectors, Inc.

   Available to members only. Applications to:-
   N.A.W.C.C.
   P.O. Box 33
   Columbia, Pa., 17512

Antiquarian Horology.
  Available to members only. Applications to:-
  The Antiquarian Horological Society
  New House
  High Street
  Ticehurst
  Wadhurst
  Sussex TN5 7AL, England

American Horologist & Jeweler
  2403 Champa Street
  Denver, Colorado 80205

CROWNED HEADS OF ENGLAND

Accession	Monarch	Died	House	
1189	Richard I	1199	Plantagenet	
1199	John	1216	"	
1216	Henry III	1272	"	
1272	Edward I	1307	"	
1307	Edward II	1327	"	Murdered
1327	Edward III	1377	"	
1377	Richard II	1400	"	Dethroned 1399. Murdered
1399	Henry IV	1413	Lancaster	
1413	Henry V	1422	"	
1422	Henry VI	1471	"	Deposed 1461
1461	Edward IV	1483	York	
1483	Edward V	1483	"	Murdered
1483	Richard III	1485	"	Slain at Battle of Bosworth

End of the Middle Ages

Accession	Monarch	Died	House	
1485	Henry VII	1509	Tudor	
1509	Henry VIII	1547	"	
1547	Edward VI	1553	"	
1553	Lady Jane Grey	1554	"	Beheaded. Reigned 9 days during 1553
1553	Mary	1558	"	
1558	Elizabeth I	1603	"	
1603	James I	1625	Stuart	James VI of Scotland
1625	Charles I	1649	"	Beheaded
1649	Commonwealth	1658		Oliver Cromwell Protector
1658	"			Richard Cromwell Protector Resigned 1660
1660	Charles II	1685	Stuart	
1685	James II	1701	"	Abdicated 1688
1688	William II & Mary (Prince of Orange)	1702	"	Mary died 1694
1702	Anne	1714	"	
1714	George I	1727	Hanover	
1727	George II	1760	"	
1760	George III	1820	"	
1820	George IV	1830	"	
1830	William IV	1837	"	
1837	Victoria	1901	"	
1901	Edward VII	1910	"	

World Time

Sundials measure solar time which is the apparent or true time, while clocks measure equal or mean time which is a solar year equally divided.

The earth rotates upon an imaginary axis that passes through the north and south poles and one revolution is equal to 360°. Lines of longitude 1° apart are drawn round the globe each line passing through the poles. One line passes through Greenwich and this is known as longitude 0° and represents Greenwich Mean Time (GMT). It has been internationally accepted as the initial meridian upon which world standard times are based. Other lines of longitude are referred to as being so many degrees east or west of Greenwich.

It takes 24 hours for the earth to rotate 360° and so 4 minutes in time = 1 degree of longitude, or every 15 degrees = 1 hour.

The direction of the earth's rotation is such that the sun rises in the east and sets in the west. The day therefore commences earlier for places in the east and later for more western locations. To calculate local time at any given Greenwich time one must add to GMT for places east of Greenwich and subtract for places west of Greenwich.

STANDARD TIMES (Corrected to September 1973)

LIST 1—PLACES FAST ON G.M.T. (mainly those EAST OF GREENWICH)

The times given }*added* to G.M.T. to give Standard Time.
below should be }*subtracted* from Standard Time to give G.M.T.:

	h	m
Aden (Southern Yemen)	03	
Admiralty Islands	10	
Afghanistan	04	30
Albania	01	
Amirante Islands	04	
Andaman Islands	05	30
Angola (Portuguese West Africa)	01	
Annobon Island	01	
Arabian Emirates, Federation of	04	
Australia		
Australian Capital Territory	10	
New South Wales	10	
Northern Territory	09	30
Queensland	10	
South Australia	09	30
Tasmania	10	
Victoria	10	
Western Australia	08	
Austria	01	
Balearic Islands	01	
Bangladesh	06	
Belgium	01	

	h	m
Botswana, Republic of	02	
British New Guinea	10	
Brunei	08	
Bulgaria	02	
Burma	06	30
Burundi	02	
Cambodia	07	
Cameroun Republic	01	
Caroline Islands, east of long. E. 160°	12	
west of long. E. 160°	10	
Truk, Ponape	11	
Central African Republic	01	
Ceylon (Sri Lanka)	05	30
Chad	01	
Chagos Archipelago	05	
Chatham Islands	12	45
China	08	
Christmas Island, Indian Ocean	07	
Cocos Keeling Islands	06	30
Comoro Islands	03	
Congo Republic	01	
Corsica	01	

STANDARD TIMES (Corrected to September 1973)
LIST I—*(continued)*

	h m		h m
Crete	.02	Guam	.10
Cyprus	.02		
Cyrenaica	.02	Holland (The Netherlands)	.01
Czechoslovakia	.01	Hong Kong	.08
		Hungary	.01
Dohomey, Republic of	.01		
Denmark	.01	India	.05 30
Egypt (United Arab Republic)	.02	Indonesia, Republic of	
Ellice Islands	.12	Bali, Bangka, Billiton, Java, Lombok, Madura, Sumatra	.07
Equatorial Guinea, Republic of	.01	Bornco, Celebes, Flores, Sumba, Sumbawa, Timor	.08
Estonia	.03	Aru, Kei, Moluccas, Tanimbar, West Irian	.09
Ethiopia	.03		
		Iran	.03 30
Fernando Poo	.01	Iraq	.03
Fiji	.12	Irish Republic	.01
Finland	.02	Israel	.02
Formosa (Taiwan)	.08	Italy	.01
France	.01		
French Territory of the Afars and Issas	.03	Japan	.09
Friendly Islands	.13	Jordan	.02
Gabon	.01	Kamchatka Peninsula	.12
Germany	.01	Kenya	.03
Gibraltar	.01	Korea	.09
Gilbert and Ellice Islands	.12		
Greece	.02		

STANDARD TIMES LIST I—*(continued)*

	h m
Rwanda	02
Ryukya Islands	09
Sakhalin	11
Santa Cruz Islands	11
Sardinia	01
Saudi Arabia	02
Schouten Islands	09
Seychelles	04
Siam (Thailand)	07
Sicily	01
Singapore	07 30
Socotra	03
Solomon Islands	11
Somali Republic	03
South Africa, Republic of	02
Southern Yemen	03
South Vietnam	08
South West Africa	02
Spain	01
Spitsbergen (Svalbard)	01
Sri Lanka (Ceylon)	05 30
Sudan, Republic of	02
Swaziland	02
Sweden	01
Switzerland	01
Syria (Syrian Arab Republic)	02
Taiwan (Formosa)	08
Tanzania	03
Thailand	07
Timor	08

	h m
Tonga Islands	13
Tripolitania	02
Truk	11
Tunisia	01
Turkey	02
Uganda	03
Union of Soviet Socialist Republics	
west of long. E. 40°	03
long. E. 40° to E. 52° 30′	04
long. E. 52° 30′ to E. 67° 30′	05
long. E. 67° 30′ to E. 82° 30′	06
long. E. 82° 30′ to E. 97° 30′	07
long. E. 97° 30′ to E. 112° 30′	08
long. E. 112° 30′ to E. 127° 30′	09
long. E. 127° 30′ to E. 142° 30′	10
long. E. 142° 30′ to E. 157° 30′	11
long. E. 157° 30′ to E. 172° 30′	12
east of long. E. 172° 30′	13
Vietnam, North	07
South	08
Wrangell Island	13
Yugoslavia	01
Zaire	
Kinshasa, Mbandaka	01
Orientale, Kivu, Katanga, Kasai	02
Zambia, Republic of	02

STANDARD TIMES (Corrected to September 1973)

LIST II—PLACES NORMALLY KEEPING G.M.T.

Algeria	Gambia	Ifni	Mali	St. Helena	Tangier
Ascension Island	Ghana	Ireland, Northern	Mauritania	Sao Tome	Togo Republic
Canary Islands	Great Britain	Ivory Coast	Morocco	Senegal	Tristan da Cunha
Channel Islands	Guinea Republic	Liberia	Principe	Sierra Leone	Upper Volta
Faeroes, The	Iceland	Maderia	Rio de Ore	Spanish Sahara	

LIST III—PLACES SLOW ON G.M.T. (WEST OF GREENWICH)

The times given ⎰ *subtracted* from G.M.T. to give Standard Time.
below should be ⎱ *added* to Standard Time to give G.M.T.

	h	m
Argentina	.03	
Austral Islands	.10	
Azores	.01	
Bahamas	.05	
Barbados	.04	
Belize	.06	
Bermuda	.04	
Bolivia	.04	
Brazil, eastern	.03	
Territory of Acre	.05	
western	.04	
British Antarctic Territory	.03	

	h	m
Canada		
Alberta	.07	
British Columbia	.08	
Labrador	.04	
Manitoba	.06	
New Brunswick	.04	
Newfoundland	.03	30
Northwest Territories		
east of ong. W. 68°	.04	
long. W. 68° to W. 85°	.05	
long. W. 85° to W. 102°	.06	
west of long. W. 102°	.07	
Nova Scotia	.04	

STANDARD TIMES (Corrected to September 1973)

LIST III—(*continued*)

	h m
Ontario, east of long. W. 90°	.05
west of long. W. 90°	.06
Prince Edward Island	.04
Quebec, east of long. W. 63°	.04
west of long. W. 73°	.05
Saskatchewan	
east of long. W. 106°	.06
west of long. W. 106°	.07
Yukon, east of long. W. 138°	.08
west of long. W. 138°	.09
Cape Verde Islands	.02
Cayman Islands	.05
Chile	.04
Christmas Island, Pacific Ocean	.10
Colombia	.05
Cook Islands, except Niue	.10 30
Costa Rica	.06
Cuba	.05
Curacao Island	.04
Dominican Republic	.05
Dutch Guiana (Surinam)	.03 30
Easter Island (I. de Pascua)	.07
Ecuador	.05

	h m
Falkland Islands	.04
Fanning Island	.10
Fernando de Noranha Island	.02
French Guiana	.03
Galapagos Islands	.05
Greenland, Scoresby Sound	.02
Angmagssalik and west coast	.03
Thule area	.04
Grenada	.04
Guadeloupe	.04
Guatemala	.06
Guiana, Dutch	.03 30
French	.04
Guyana, Republic of	.03 45
Haiti	.05
Honduras	.06
Honduras, British (Belize)	.06
Jamaica	.05
Jan Mayen Island	.01
Johnston Island	.10
Juan Fernandez Islands	.04

	h	m
Leeward Islands	.04	
Low Archipelago	.10	
Marquesas Islands	.09	30
Martinique	.04	
Mexico	.06	
Midway Islands	.11	
Miquelon	.03	
Nicaragua	.06	
Niue Island	.11	
Panama Canal Zone	.05	
Panama, Republic of	.05	
Paraguay	.04	
Peru	.05	
Portuguese Guinea	.01	
Puerto Rico	.04	
Rarotonga	.10	30
St. Pierre and Miquelon	.03	
Salvador, El	.06	
Samoa	.11	
Society Islands	.10	
South Georgia	.02	
Surinam (Dutch Guiana)	.03	30
Tobago	.04	
Trinidade Island, South Atlantic	.02	

	h	m
Trinidad	.04	
Tuamotu Archipelago	.10	
Tubuai Islands	.10	
Turks and Caicos Islands	.05	
United States of America		
Alabama	.06	
Alaska, east of long. W. 137°	.08	
long. W. 137° to W. 141°	.09	
long. W. 141° to W. 161°	.10	
long. W. 161° to W. 172° 30	.11	
Aleutian Islands	.11	
Arizona	.07	
Arkansas	.06	
California	.08	
Colorado	.07	
Connecticut	.05	
Delaware	.05	
District of Columbia	.05	
Florida	.05	
Georgia	.05	
Hawaii	.10	
Idaho	.07	
Illinois	.06	
Indiana	.05	
Iowa	.06	
Kansas	.06	
Kentucky	.05	
Louisiana	.06	
Maine	.05	
Maryland	.05	

United States of America (continued)

	h	m
Massachusetts		.05
Michigan		.05
Minnesota		.06
Mississippi		.06
Missouri		.06
Montana		.07
Nebraska		.06
Nevada		.08
New Hampshire		.05
New Jersey		.05
New Mexico		.07
New York		.05
North Carolina		.05
North Dakota		.06
Ohio		.05
Oklahoma		.06
Oregon		.08
Pennsylvania		.05
Rhode Island		.05

	h	m
South Carolina		.05
South Dakota, eastern part		.06
western part		.07
Tennessee		.06
Texas		.06
Utah		.07
Vermont		.05
Virginia		.05
Washington, D.C.		.05
Washington		.08
West Virginia		.05
Wisconsin		.06
Wyoming		.07
Uruguay		.03
Venezuela		.04
Virgin Islands		
Windward Islands		.04

The Date or Calendar Line is an arbitrary line, on either side of which the date differs by one day; when crossing this line on a westerly course, the date must be advanced one day; when crossing it on an easterly course, the date must be put back one day. The line is a modification of the line of the 180th meridian, and is drawn so as to include, as far as possible, islands of any one group, etc., on the same side of the line. It may be traced by starting at the South Pole and joining up the the following positions:

Lat.	S. 51.0	S. 45.0	S. 15.0	S. 5.0	N. 48.0	N. 53.0	N. 65.5
Long.	180.0	W. 172.5	W. 172.5	180.0	180.0	E. 170.0	W. 169.0

thence through the middle of the Diomede Islands to Lat. N. 68°.0, Long. W. 169°.0, passing east of Ostrov Vrangelya (Wrangel Island) to Lat. N. 75°.0, Long. 180°.0, and thence to the North Pole.

ACKNOWLEDGMENTS

Figures 7, 8 and 11 by courtesy of the Science Museum, South Kensington, London SW7 2DD, England.

Figures 14-18, 55 and 71 by courtesy of G.E. Marsh, 32A The Square, Winchester, Hampshire SO 23 9EX, England.

Figures 19-21, 101, 103-106, 108, 109, 113 and 114 by courtesy of the Hunter Collection of Clocks of the Illinois State Museum, Springfield, Illinois 62706.

Figures 27-29, 31, 32, 34-36, 48, 50-54, 58, 76, 78, 80, 83, 87, 90, 95 and 98 by courtesy of Kingston Antiques, 138 London Road, Kingston upon Thames, Surrey, England.

Figures 30 and 100 by courtesy of Strike One, 1A Camden Walk, London, N.1., England.

Figures 33, 47, 57, 59, 99 and 115-126 by courtesy of Messrs. King & Chasemore, The Pulborough Saleroom, Pulborough, Sussex RH 20 1AJ, England.

Figures 44, 45, 60-63, 65-70, 72, 73, 77, 79, 81, 82, 84, 86 and 88 by courtesy of Garrad & Co. Ltd., The Crown Jewellers, 112 Regent St., London W1A 2JJ, England.

Figures 46, 56, 85, 89, 91-94, 96 and 97 by courtesy of D. Bouldstringe Ltd., 47 Lower Belgrave St., Eaton Square, London, S.W.1., England.

Figures 49, 64 and 74 by courtesy of Meyrick Neilson of Tetbury Ltd., Market Place, Tetbury, Gloucestershire 6L8 8DF, England.

Figures 102, 107, 110 and 112 by courtesy of Sotheby Parke Bernet Inc., 980 Madison Avenue, New York, N.Y. 10021.

The author wishes to acknowledge the kindness of those who loaned the above photographs for use as illustrations, and to thank Mr. Richard Lonergan for producing the drawings.

INDEX

253

254

256